Aspects of the Cult of Cybele and Attis on the Monuments from the Republic of Croatia

Aleksandra Nikoloska

BAR International Series 2086
2010

Published in 2016 by
BAR Publishing, Oxford

BAR International Series 2086

Aspects of the Cult of Cybele and Attis on the Monuments from the Republic of Croatia

ISBN 978 1 4073 0562 2

© A Nikoloska and the Publisher 2010

The author's moral rights under the 1988 UK Copyright,
Designs and Patents Act are hereby expressly asserted.

All rights reserved. No part of this work may be copied, reproduced, stored,
sold, distributed, scanned, saved in any form of digital format or transmitted
in any form digitally, without the written permission of the Publisher.

BAR Publishing is the trading name of British Archaeological Reports (Oxford) Ltd.
British Archaeological Reports was first incorporated in 1974 to publish the BAR
Series, International and British. In 1992 Hadrian Books Ltd became part of the BAR
group. This volume was originally published by Archaeopress in conjunction with
British Archaeological Reports (Oxford) Ltd / Hadrian Books Ltd, the Series principal
publisher, in 2010. This present volume is published by BAR Publishing, 2016.

Printed in England

PUBLISHING

BAR titles are available from:

	BAR Publishing
	122 Banbury Rd, Oxford, OX2 7BP, UK
EMAIL	info@barpublishing.com
PHONE	+44 (0)1865 310431
FAX	+44 (0)1865 316916
	www.barpublishing.com

For my parents

Map showing the sites mentioned in text. Inset: location of Croatia.

CONTENTS

INTRODUCTION 3

THE CULT IN THE TERRITORY OF THE REPUBLIC OF CROATIA, GENERAL OVERVIEW 6

MYSTERY ASPECTS OF THE CULT 14

ICONOGRAPHY 20

THE FRESCO FROM ZADAR AND THE MOTIF OF THE CORYBANTES 31

CONCLUSION 40

CATALOGUE 43

ILLUSTRATIONS 64

ABBREVIATIONS 100

WORKS CITED 101

INTRODUCTION

From time eternal, the omnipotent Great Goddess answers to the sound of tympana and cymbals imitating the roar of the wolves and lions. She dwells high in the mountains and woods, reigning over untameable natural forces, but also over social order and fortified cities. Her character is stable, but dual – She is the Earth, permanent and ever present; her domain both life and death. As opposed to the immutable Goddess, Attis is time and again followed by metamorphosis, whether in myth, turning from a beautiful shepherd into a pine tree, or in the religious awareness of the worshippers, evolving from a eunuch priest of Cybele into a demiurge. Their relation is polyvalent; he is her lover and her son, containing also the paternal aspect. Although privileged, Attis, in relation to Cybele was a lower ranked deity and in early times never worshipped independently from her. Attis completes the significance of the Goddess in the way that he represents the active element of the creative cycle of nature, while she is the bearer of the passive, stable element. They stand in synergy transmitting the idea of creation, death, and rebirth, offering in that way hope of salvation of the souls of their worshippers in the afterlife. The *galloi* and Attis as their prototype were not enthusiastically accepted in the Greek world. The Romans were also highly selective considering the choice of rituals when they Romanised the already Hellenised cult from Pessinus in Republican times.

In the cultures of the Near East and the Mediterranean, the Great Goddess marked her presence as a central religious figure for thousands of years. It was Mother Earth that contained and gave life, governed the fertile ground and followed the rhythm of the moon and vegetation. By the second millennium B.C. the cult of the Great Goddess began to expand in many locations in Asia Minor and Syria. It is considered that in this period the name, epithets, and attributes of Cybele were defined.[1] With the entrance of the Indo-Europeans on the religious scene of Anatolia, the autochthonic Goddess does not cease to exist, but assimilates and adapts.[2] She is symbolically adjoined to the King of Heavens as his spouse and becomes the Queen and Mother of Gods and of the people and animals that came out of the earth. In the Hittite pantheon it was Kubaba who was the cardinal female deity with her cult centred in the city of Karkemish.[3] The cult of the Great Kubaba spread over Asia Minor in the first millennium and occupied a key position in the spiritual systems of this region. Among scholars, the thought that the Phrygian Cybele is a direct successor of the Hittite Kubaba is generally accepted. This transition is best seen in the development of the name of the Goddess,[4] but also through some iconographical pointers that point to this fact.[5] In the late eighth century there was an alliance between Karkemish and Gordion, and right through that strong cultural exchange the cult was adopted among the Phrygians,[6] the greatest worshippers of the Goddess. According to the Greek inscriptions, they called her $Κυβήβη$;[7] she enjoyed the status of a national deity and was the only one anthropomorphically depicted. Although Gordion was the main political centre of Phrygia, the main centre of the cult of Cybele was Pessinus, the holy city by the mythical river Sangarius. The cult was part of the history of Pessinus even from the Bronze Age where the black uniconical meteorite, the idol through which she was worshipped had the meaning of an omphalos, designating the city as a spiritual Centrum.[8] Vast numbers of statues, terracottas, and lines written in the ancient scriptures indicate the deep traces this goddess left over the religious conscience of the Phrygians. In different regions and periods Cybele was identified and connected to many deities, but the basic concept of the omnipresent Earth Goddess and Mother of Gods (*Mater Theon*) remained the same, up to as late as the very beginnings of her comprehension. In Asia Minor Cybele was understood above all as the Mistress of wild animals (*Potnia theron*) and as Mother of mountain peeks. She was guarded by fearsome lions, her loyal protectors, above which she has absolute power. As founder and protector of cities, Goddess of fertility, but also as chthonic Goddess of destruction, Cybele carried within her structure strong ambivalent characteristics. Her sanctuaries, apart from being built within the city walls, were erected high in the mountains, constantly reminding of her mythical abode.

When the religious idea of the Great Goddess spread across the Near East and the Mediterranean, many female deities with common elements appeared in different parts of this region, but also certain types of male gods following the goddesses appeared, creating in that way complete mythological entireties. By ways of syncretism and identification with these deities, the cult of Cybele and Attis steadily evolved, simultaneously enriching the mythology and rituality. All of the mythological cycles with which Cybele and Attis came into contact have common elements through which a certain conceptual subject can be perceived. It is a way of comprehending, accepting, and presenting a religious idea, equal and comparable in many cultures – the death of a god and his rebirth, a model out of which a paradigm of ritual practice derives. Gods die so they can achieve immortality, reflected in the eternal cycle of vicissitude. It is, in fact, the blessing of the holy unity with the Goddess, achieved by initiation through the sphere of death and through hypnotic frenzies and mutilation which offer godly privileges. The sacrifice of the primary instinct is presented as one of the ways of reaching the absolute divine. Attis castrates himself and that is the only way to maintain his promise of devotion to the Great Mother.

---

[1] Vermaseren 1977a, 16, 17.
[2] Gimbutas 1989, 318.
[3] Albright 1929, 229.
[4] Albright 1929; Diakonoff 1977.
[5] Naumann 1983, 30, 31.
[6] Rein 1996, 224-227.
[7] Vermaseren 1977a, 21.
[8] Sanders 1981, 276.

Cybele was evoked by hypnotic music and orgiastic ceremonies, followed by ecstatic dance and the emasculation of her priests – the *galloi*. The orgiastic element, the eunuchism, the initiatory – mystic and the soteriological character carried great importance in the ritual, mutually creating a complementary net. However, all these elements were independent from each other and had separate developments during the integration of the cult in different religious systems.

Key characteristics of the cult are the power to assimilate and the syncretistic nature of the bearer gods. Cybele underwent an intensive process of Hellenisation, therefore it is impossible to distinguish the Phrygian aspects from those gained in Greece. The ancient Greeks met Cybele in Asia Minor and in her figure recognised the Great Goddess from Crete, which in many ways helped the acceptance of the cult.[9] She was identified with the Greek maternal goddesses, Rea and Demeter. In Greece, Attis was not accepted with delight. He was only venerated in Piraeus where the spring festivities of *Attideia* were held. There the cult was established by the community of foreigners, *thiasotai*.[10] By its content, the cult of the Great Mother in Greece is an exceptionally interesting and nonetheless complex system including Anatolian and autochthonic Greek elements. By the process of migrating myths the Bronze Age religion of Hattusa and Ugarit spread its branches and in the so-called 'orientalizing period' greatly contributed to the formation of Greek culture. So, certain motifs of the myth and cult of the Great Mother made a transition from the East and blended into the mythological and ritual systems of the Greeks.[11]

There is a distinct polarity of the cultic image of the Great Mother, who was a protectress of the legal order and the social organisation, while on the other hand demanding completely the opposite, ecstatic and wild ritual practices. Resurrecting the wild rhythm of nature was needed in order to redefine the social order.[12] The duality, whether ritualistic or iconographical, was constantly presented by the figure of the Great Mother Goddess. Fundamentally, it reaches to the elementary ambivalence – the opposition of life and death, clearly visible in her mystery rituals. If we observe the ritual practice of the Greeks in the early periods, we notice that the local concept of the Mother Goddess had roots as deep as the Neolithic spiritual tradition. Here, the Great Mother was a pastoral deity, rising each year from the earth, summoned by the population in times when she was most needed. She provided water and rich crops; therefore spring and summer were the periods of the year when her presence was most strongly felt. The understanding of the cultic tradition of the Great Mother in Greece relates to the study of etiological myths, considering that the connection between myth and ritual is inseparable. Exactly from the myths we can perceive the background of the foundation of the local festivals, which were in fact the main ways of celebrating the gods, set in the periods when the help of a certain deity was essential and necessary. Etiological myths, and festivals such as Galaxia and Kronia help us in many aspects to understand the cult tradition of the Great Mother in Greece.[13]

The Romans, just like the Greeks, took over the cult from Asia Minor, although not through a gradual cultural interchange, but with an official visit advised by the Sibylline books. The importation of the Great Mother within the roman pantheon in the year 204 B.C. preceded a long tradition of accepting foreign deities that acted upon a progressive modification of Republican religion.[14] But the Romans did not celebrate the Goddess in the way the Greeks did. In her honour the Megalensia was held,[15] the only roman festival with a foreign name derived from the Greek name of the Goddess – Μήτηρ μεγάλη.[16] Megalensia was an exclusively patrician festival, completely adapted to the Roman customs of Republican times, when the cult was in the hands of the aristocracy. Only later, during the March festivals, was the Phrygian religious concept of the divine vicissitude as a guarantee of fertility and rebirth actualised. In such manner, despite the changes undergone by the cult in order to adjust to the conservative republican taste, the cult succeeded in transmitting certain oriental elements and to infect the West with cathartic rituals. The typical Roman way of celebrating Cybele, the Megalensia, was completely replaced by these public ceremonies.[17] March rituals were a clear reflection of the Phrygian element of the cult, with Attis as a central figure.

Rome imbued Cybele with greatness and an international reputation. She had her dwelling on the Palatine and was highly respected among Roman aristocracy, poets and the emperors. With Romanization, the cult of Cybele and Attis reached all the western provinces, where it followed an autochthonic development influenced by local divinities and traditional spiritual concepts. That is how the cult gained certain different attributes in different parts of the Empire, adorned with elements familiar to the local population and their traditional needs. Nevertheless, the basic idea remained the same. Although controversial in terms of ritual, the cult of the Great Mother lasted until it succumbed to the fierce attacks of the Christians. The last *taurobolium* that we know of was held in 390[18] while the cult was officially terminated in 391/2 during the time of Theodosius when, together with all pagan temples, the Metroons were also closed down.[19]

The cult of Cybele and Attis is a spiritual phenomenon of wide chronological and geographical range. There is abundant documentation of its existence, but even more numerous are the works of scholars engaged in the

---

[9] Burkert 1979, 103.
[10] Sfameni Gasparro 1983, 49-52.
[11] Burkert 1987b, 13-14.
[12] Burkert 1983, 134.
[13] Robertson 1996.
[14] Gruen 1990.
[15] Turcan 1996a, 38-40.
[16] Ciceron, *De har. resp.*, 12, 24.
[17] Vermaseren 1977a, 113-124.
[18] CIL 6.512.
[19] Burkert 1987a, 53.

interpretation of the cult and the divine figures around it. It is a field of interest for linguists, classicists, archaeologists, historians and art historians, ethnologists, and even psychoanalysts. To try to display all the aspects of the cult, its rituality and manifestation in iconography and epigraphy is a hard assignment. Countless studies have been made trying to portray the character and evolution of the cult of the Phrygian Great Goddess, the timeless Mother of Gods, and her paredros Attis. The work presented here is another interpretative drop in the vast cultural sea that these deities have left behind, focusing on one particular corner of the Roman Empire.

THE CULT IN THE TERRITORY OF THE REPUBLIC OF CROATIA, GENERAL OVERVIEW

The conditions of acceptance, spread, and prevalence of the Cult

The cult of the Mother Goddess in the provinces of Illyricum is attested only in the Roman period, a very important fact that helps postulate the preliminary parameters in the reconstruction of the form manifested here. The beginning of the acceptance of the Great Mother and her paredros Attis happened almost simultaneously in Dalmatia, as well as in Pannonia and Histria, which in that period was part of the Xth Roman region *Venetia et Histria*. This is the time of the early Empire and the rapid international acceptance of the Romanized cult of the Phrygian Great Goddess. However, the cult that was celebrated in these parts was only an echo of its greatness enjoyed in Rome. Even though it was a foreign cult, its acceptance was not the result of radical changes but of the gradual assimilation of Roman religiosity with the spiritual needs of the local population. With time, Roman religiosity overcame its autochthonic traditional ways. Nevertheless, with it came the oriental way of rituality and also the mysteries that were part of the Mother Goddess religious system. The influences that acted upon the adoption of the cult were Italic and came directly with immigrants, trade, or via the army. There was also an oriental influence because of the existence of certain oriental ethnic groups. One of the main routes of the arrival of the cult was Aquilea, however we must not forget the eastern routes and the open communication with the Danubian provinces. The prior affiliation of the Goddess with the eastern religious systems greatly affected the later local development of the cult in Illyricum, especially in Pannonia.

What was the autochthonic spiritual tradition that Cybele and Attis could have continued? Certainly, the *Nesactium* cult most vividly displays the local prehistoric heritage. *Nesactium* was not only the administrative, but also the spiritual centre of Histria up until 177 B.C. when *Pola* (today's Pula) prevailed.[20] The *Nesactium* sculptures show that here the Goddess Mother was celebrated from the Neolithic period and that rituals of a supposed mystery character were also performed. Apart from the abstract geometric motifs, we also find interesting figurative ones that can be comparatively analyzed with the figures from Çatal Hüyük.[21] Above all, there is a kourotrophos female figure with overemphasized vulva (fig. 1). The conceptual idea of this sculpture is the same as the Great Goddess from Çatal Hüyük (fig. 2). They both are giving birth and their nutritive function is emphasized. Only the attributes referring to the ruling positions of the Nesactian Goddess are missing. The Double head (fig. 3) is another link between the cultic picture of the Anatolian and the *Nesactian* spiritual heritage. There are several examples of two figures melding into one from Çatal Hüyük (fig. 4);[22] the *Nesactian* figure also hints at a local awareness of the duality concept. Duality is an important element of the Mother Goddess religion contained in the basic idea that this cult transmitted, and is recognizable in the cult iconography. In mythology the concept of duality is expressed through the image of the androgen Agdistis.[23] The idea of duality is especially reflected in the mystery religions as well as in Gnosticism in later times.[24]

The Goddess's character as a protector of natural fertility has most certainly helped in her local acceptance. Often in the cult's iconography we can see symbols such as the *cornucopia* – or ears of corn. In Rome the Great Mother was syncretized with Agraria,[25] and in Aquilea with Ceres.[26] In Histria and especially in Liburnia, numerous autochthonic fertility goddesses were worshipped who were related to the organization of local society and the status of local women. It is believed that Liburnian society was oriented towards agrarian economy and that women had distinguished roles.[27] These conditions more that sufficed to permit Magna Mater to intervene in the Liburnian religious system. It is difficult to be specific about the autochthonic goddesses with whom Magna Mater came into contact and with whom she identified during the process of her local acceptance. Inscriptions that tell us about their presence are limited to certain small regions and do not provide much information about their characteristics. We know even less about their imagery. One of the goddesses worshipped in *Nesactium* in Roman times was Eia,[28] connected with Cybele on several levels. This goddess of sea and earth was also protector of mental and physical health.[29] The Great Mother Cybele likewise had attributes of personal protection, including against madness. The ambivalence of this particular characteristic is that she herself had the capacity to inflict madness. Another common characteristic of these two goddesses is the identification with Bona Dea.[30] Latra is a goddess attested to on most

---

[20] Starac 1999, 8-9.
[21] Kukoč 1987; Kovač 1992; The concept of the Great Mother is traced back to the Neolithic culture of Çatal Hüyük where she was the main deity and abundantly evidenced in the finds. Certainly, the most famous is the Throne-Seated Goddess with crown on head and surrounded by panthers. Her high-ranking status and fructiferous power is expressed. It is thought to date from the period that the pattern of Cybele's iconography appeared.
[22] Meskell 1998, 49-50.
[23] Agdistis, the primordial androgen with chthonic elements, was a figure with a special position in the mythological tradition of the cult. It is a reflection of the coexisting oppositions, of the united cosmological principals and absoluteness, therefore of fertility and procreation. The androgen god is self-sufficient and auto regenerative (Zuntz 1971, 15). It is a pictorial way of representing the union of the Mother with the male principal. Agdistis was known not only in Asia Minor, but also in Greece as late as the 4th century B.C. It was identified with *Meter theon*, while the name Agdistis remained one of the Goddess's many epithets (Sfameni Gasparro 1985, 34).
[24] Reitzenstein 1978, 83.
[25] Graillot 1912, 118.
[26] Vermaseren 1978, 220; Sfameni Gasparro 1985, 84.
[27] Alföldy 1961; Kuntić-Makvić 1982, 156; Kurilić 1994, 56.
[28] Girardi – Jurkić 1999, 1.3.1-5.
[29] Šašel Kos 1999, 68.
[30] Brouwer 1978; Šašel Kos 1999, 68.

monuments from Liburnian sites, especially in Nedin, where there was even a temple dedicated to her. Latra, as well as Venus Anzotica and Iria, was a chthonic goddess.[31] We know of a statue of Cybele with a snake from *Nesactium* from the second century A.D. (figs. 5, 6), which can point to a possible continuation of prehistoric chthonic religious ideas. Undoubtedly, the Celtic Matres Magnae attested in Dalmatia had also many similarities with the Phrygian goddess.[32] As for the deities from the wider area, Noreia, the main goddess of Noricum and the personification of the province is the goddess that had the most similar features with Magna Mater. Aside from the fact that Noreia was not an autochthonic deity, but a typical Romanized *Genius loci*, she can be connected to the Great Mother on various grounds. First, there is the maternal factor, second, there is the dual nature in the sphere of life and death, and third, there is the iatric capacity. Noreia was celebrated by strangers as well as by the Romanized population. This particular deity was identified with Isis and there is an assumption that there was a male consort named Casuontanus present by her side.[33]

Šašel Kos points out that Cybele overpowered the autochthonous Liburnian goddesses of fertility.[34] Having in mind Cybele's strong syncretistic power, and the adaptability of the cult, it is most likely that she sublimed their cults in her own religious system. The spirituality that she offered was more complex and hence richer with divine offerings. The figure of the Great Mother contained some of the features of the Liburnian goddesses, and therefore the rituality which they required.

The questions about the manifested form of the cult in this region, as well as the way of its local development will be answered gradually by sifting through the material legacy. The most numerous finds come from Dalmatia, among them many inscriptions and ex-votos that reveal important pieces of the puzzle. We notice that the worshippers of the cult were mainly women, or family groups. Among the dedicants we also come across freedmen, with both Greek and oriental names. Inscriptions from Histria are rare. Except those with mention of *dendrophoroi*, we know only the inscription of Felicula, daughter of K. Valerius Optatus from Jesenovik (fig. 7),[35] who dedicated an altar to the Great Mother but also worshipped Iria.[36] We find the same situation in Pannonia, where only one epigraphical find is documented.[37] The inscription was found in Sisak (Roman *Siscia*) and it stands as further proof of the presence of the college of *dendrophoroi*.

The Goddess's name used in these parts had only its Roman form – Magna Mater. Although the Phrygian form of the name is not attested, there is a possibility that the Goddess's name was known differently. The inscription from *Salona*, which refers to the building of a sanctuary, bears a written vow addressed to a goddess named *dea barbarica* (fig. 8).[38] It is suspected that this epithet may have belonged to Cybele and relates to the goddess's origin. This fragmented inscription is dated to the early first century A.D., but the possibility that it originates from Republican times is not excluded.[39] If there was reliable proof that this epithet referred to Cybele, than it would be the earliest document testifying to this cult in Dalmatia. However, *dea barbarica* is also a deity from Galia[40] and very likely familiar in these parts, although not proven. If this inscription applied to Cybele then it might also serve as a sign that the Goddess's original Phrygian character was known. Nevertheless, in absence of suitable evidence this stands only as an assumption. Two freedmen with Greek cognomens are mentioned on the inscription in question – *Phileros* and *(H)imeros*, which is not certain proof that they were of oriental origin, especially having in mind that these kinds of names were often given to slaves. It is possible that these freedmen were in fact *seviri*, in which case this inscription will be the oldest document of the sevirate in *Salona*.[41] There is an inscription from Celeia dedicated to the Great Mother with the epithet *Blaundiae*, which is connected with the Phrygian town Blaundus[42] and can be used as another pointer that the Phrygian origin of the Goddess was known in the provinces where the cult arrived during Romanization.

The Great Goddess in Dalmatia was also known by the epithet *Augusta*, as written in the inscription field of the *tabula ansata* from *Senia*, with the dedication Verridia Psyche (fig. 9).[43] This epithet can mostly be found on inscriptions from North Africa, and judging by the gentilitium *Veridius* it can be supposed that the woman who dedicated this altar had an African origin.[44] The epithet *Augusta* is usually connected with the autochthonous goddesses, as well as with ones of Greek or Roman origin,[45] while it was never attributed to oriental deities. In the later period of the Empire, especially in the provinces, this epithet lost its primary meaning and was usually used to denote the supremacy of a certain deity.[46]

---

[31] Medini 1984b, 223-244.
[32] Šašel Kos 1999, 89.
[33] Šašel Kos 1999, 36, 40.
[34] 1999, 90.
[35] Degrassi 1933, 381; Degrassi 1936, 198; Swoboda 1969, 207, n° 19; Degrassi 1970, 625; Vermaseren 1978, n° 250; Girardi – Jurkić 1999, 3.8.2.
[36] The same person dedicated an altar to Iria; see Girardi – Jurkić 1999, 1.6.1.
[37] CIL III 10853; Kukoljević 1873, 142; Graillot 1912; 487; Selem 1980, 201, 8; Tóth 1989, 10.

[38] CIL III 14663,2; Graillot 1912, 493; Medini 1981b, n° 30; Šašel Kos 1999, 82.
[39] The archaic form *coer(averunt)* offers the possibility of earlier dating; see Šašel Kos 1999, 84.
[40] Medini 1981b, 386.
[41] Šašel Kos 1999, 84.
[42] Swoboda 1969, 8; Vermaseren 1989, 83.
[43] Degmedžić 1952, 251-4 fig.1; Medini 1978, 736-737 pl.148 fig 2; Medini 1981b, n°3; Vermaseren 1989, n° 128.
[44] Glavičić 1994, 63-65.
[45] Some of these goddesses are Belestis (Šašel Kos 1999, 21); Eia (Girardi – Jurkić 1999, 1.3.1.-3.); Trita (Girardi – Jurkić 1999, 1.12.1.); Ica (Girardi – Jurkić 1999, 1.14.1.); Flora (Girardi – Jurkić 1999, 2.20.1.); Nemesis (Girardi – Jurkić 1999, 3.6.1.).
[46] Šašel Kos 1999, 75-76.

J. Medini distinguished the development of the cult in the province of Dalmatia into three periods. The first period is from the first century until the second half of the second century, when the cult spread from *Salona* to *Senia* and *Arba*. The worshippers of the cult in this period were mainly representatives of the lower society stratum – freedmen, slaves and soldiers.[47] From the archaeological and epigraphical record, we can confirm that there were buildings involved with the cult in several locations. During the excavations in *Senia*,[48] the walls of a Metroon were found near the Cathedral. The temple adjoined a house from the same period, and, apparently, they were correlated in some way (fig. 10). It is possible that the house belonged to the temple priest. In the same area a statue of the Goddess was found that was also associated with the temple, along with the mentioned inscription of Verridia Psyche, according to which it was determined that the temple was build in the second half of the first century. The temple and the house were in later times destroyed in a fire. The inscription found on the island of Rab[49] refers to T. Prusius Optatus, who wanted a porch dedicated to the Great Mother to be erected in his honour by his sister and heir Barbia Tertulla. This monument dates from the beginning of the second century at the latest.[50] H. Graillot pointed out that this porch was part of the necropolis, analogous to Phrygian monuments of a funeral character dedicated to Cybele.[51] Opposed to Graillot's opinion, Medini prefers to see the porch in relation to the sanctuary dedicated to the Goddess, plausibly located at an important town location, and that the cult came on the island with immigrants from Italy.[52] *Iader* (modern Zadar) was also an important centre of the cult in Dalmatia. The findings from *Iader* are not numerous, but very important. Alongside the inscription of the Salonitan *archigallus*,[53] a chamber in the service of the cult was found. It is of a different character than the already-mentioned cult buildings, therefore it requires different approach. *Aenona* has also offered findings connected to the cult and to the possible existence of a local Metroon, or even Attideum. Namely, a relief with an image of *Attis tristis* was found[54] that could have been a part of the temple frieze. According to other finds from *Aenona* it can be assumed that Attis had an important role in the local understanding of the afterlife. It is in *Aenona* that the largest concentration of grave appliqués with the bust of Attis has been found.

In the beginning of the second period, the cult developed a certain momentum and spread within the mainland of the province, east from the *Salona*-Glamoč line. The cult was also confirmed in smaller settlements in Dalmatia (Lepuri, Vrlika), most likely the result of an influence from the castrum in *Tilurium*, and from the one in *Burnum*. Roman spiritual trends in the provinces at the time of the Empire were widely accepted as a result of the influence of the army. The Seventh and Eleventh Roman legions were appointed in Dalmatia, among whose ranks were many orientals.[55] It is possible to recognize Attis on the tombstones of the soldiers, while in *Burnum* Forum there was certainly a building in service of the cult (fig. 11). The cult of Cybele and Attis existed here as part of the imperial cult. A reconstruction of the apsidal sanctuary on the *Burnum* Forum was confirmed, occurring after the reforms of Antonius Pius and during which an aedicule with the motif of the Mother Goddess cult was placed. This site yielded a monumental frieze with relief depiction of the mythological scene of Cybele and Attis after the castration.[56] Having in mind that the Metroon had an important position on the Forum, it is evident that the cult in *Burnum* was especially respected.

Despite the naturalistic values that the cult was offering, and onto which the local population could have responded, in this period eschatological values can also be recognized. The soteriological, and especially eschatological, elements of the cult helped increase its popularity among the local population. The notion of salvation and the afterlife in the first centuries A.D. became present, thus the need for cults that could offer these new religious experiences. The idea of the celestial immortality of the soul can be perceived on the funeral monuments on which there is an image of *Attis tristis*, often found within the territory of the Republic of Croatia. This spiritual concept was distinctively expressed on the tombstone of the young Aeronius Firmin from *Salona*, from the middle of the second century A.D.[57] Sfameni Gasparro places this concept as transitional in the process of Attis's divine transformation, which in the third, and, especially, the fourth century reached the cosmic and astral comprehension of the young god's nature.[58]

Salona was at the heart of the Mother Goddess cult in Dalmatia and offers us a truly interesting cult profile. It can be acknowledged, based on the abundance of finds, that the cult in *Salona* held a very important place as early as the first century A.D., until the predomination of the Christianity. The finds, and in particular their specificity, enables us to observe the Mother Goddess cult in *Salona* as a separate unit within the province of Dalmatia. G. Kubitschek in 1896 collected 9 inscriptions that seemed to point to the worship of the cult in

---

[47] Medini 1981b, 383-395.
[48] Degmedžić 1952, 251-262; Glavičić 1968, 22; Medini 1978, 734f; Medini 1981b, n°2; Vermaseren, 1989, n°127.
[49] CIL III 3115; Graillot 1912, n.1; Medini 1967, 48; Medini 1978, 733-734; Schillinger 1978, 55-56, 66f; Medini 1981b, n°1; Vermaseren 1989, n° 131.
[50] Medini 1981b, n°.4, 48.
[51] 1912, 494.
[52] 1981b, 198-9.
[53] CIL III 2920a; Graillot 1912, n°4, 492, n.11; Suić 1965b, 100; Medini 1981a, 15-28; Medini 1981b, n°17; Vermaseren 1989, n°141.
[54] Medini 1989b, 19-31.

[55] Medini 1981b, 387-388.
[56] Reisch 1913, 119-121, fig. 33; Schober 1923, 215; Medini 1978, 744-5, Pl. 155,1; Vermaseren 1966, 37; Vermaseren 1977a, 143; Medini 1981b, n° 24; Vermaseren 1989, n° 147.
[57] Q. Aeronio / Firmino d(e)f(uncto) / ann. XIIII mes. IIII / Q. Aeronius Crescens / Caetrania Firma paren(tes) // filio pientiss(imo) lib(ertis) lib(ertabus)q(ue) suis. Inuida Parcarum series liuorque malignus / bis septena mea[e] ruperunt stamina lucis. / Parcite iam lachrimis, miseri soliq(ue) parentes: / sat fletus uestros prima fauilla bibit. / Corpus habent cineres, animam sacer abstulit aer. (CIL III 6384, Hepding 1903, 86, 25; Graillot 1912, 493; Lagrange 1919, 475; Medini 1981b, n° 58).
[58] 1985, 98-99.

Salona.[59] Today we know of eleven out of twenty-nine private Salonitan municipal inscriptions from the first until the third century. They tell us about individuals renewing, or in some other way investing in the maintenance of the sanctuaries devoted to the Great Mother.[60] The main temple of the cult in *Salona* has never been found. This, however, is not confirmation that a building of this character did not exist, especially judging by the great importance that the cult had in the Dalmatian metropolis. There were many sanctuaries coexisting; new ones were being erected and old ones were being restored. However, if we compare the public temples from *Senia* and *Arba* that were erected in central town positions, we see that here we have a different situation. Salonitan sanctuaries were outside the city walls. However, remains of buildings that can be associated with Mother Goddess sanctuaries have not been found. We have, as yet, only epigraphical information. Analyses of the inscriptions reveal that three terms (*aedes, fanum, templum*) were used when referring to these sacral cult buildings. The engagement of *ordo decurionis* is not mentioned in any of the inscriptions; therefore, we can freely conclude that these sanctuaries were of private character.[61] *Aedes* is the term most often found on Salonitan ex-votos, and it is used to denote the temple building itself.[62] It is mentioned in the vow of Iunia Rhodine,[63] who, together with her family, renewed and expanded the sanctuary building. It can also be found on the inscription from which we read of Turranius Cronius, who, on the other hand, erected and adorned the Goddess's sanctuary.[64] This particular inscription was found near the spring of the river Iadro, and is supposed to mark the exact location of the sanctuary, although we do not have firm proof.[65] The term *aedes* is inscribed on another Salonitan vow, that of the dedicant Iulius Rufus.[66] The example from Trogir dedicated to the Great Mother (fig. 12),[67] dated to the first or second century at the latest, also reveals the existence of a sanctuary of a private character for which the same term is used. *Fanum* is another term found on the Salonitan inscriptions; on the vow of Curia Prisca,[68] and on the one set by the *cognatio*.[69] The only time that the aedicule in honour of the Great Mother was mentioned is on an inscription of Servilia Copiesilla.[70] The married couple Agrii renewed the *templum* that was ruined over time.[71] This term denotes the consecrated area, including the ground on which the temple building was erected.[72] Based on several finds, Medini established an approximate profile of these sanctuaries. The aedicule, with an inscription to a temple dedicated to the Great Mother (*templum Matris Magnae*),[73] the inscribed plate from Srinjin,[74] and some architectural elements of a supposed sanctuary of the Great Mother from the eastern part of *Salona* (fig. 13),[75] all drew his attention. According to him, the sanctuaries were small buildings with facades resembling a temple and with an epistyle with columns or antae.[76] Taking into account that none of these buildings were located, it is possible to assume that some of the inscriptions referred to monuments similar to the relief naiskoi, with an image of the Great Mother widely found, where the cult was known. Unfortunately, this kind of monument was also not found.

Two inscriptions from the wider *Salona* region tell us about supposed sanctuaries similar to the Salonitan ones. One is from Tillurium,[77] the vow of the married couple *Trebonii*, whereas the other is from near Vrlika,[78] dedicated to the Goddess by the brothers Vitalis and Maximus. There is no more information either about the engagements of the devotees or about the types of buildings in question. But we know of another neighbouring temple dedicated to Cybele – the one in Diocletian's palace. Antonio Proculiano, chancellor of Split municipality from the 16th century, registered this temple of Cybele as being opposite the one devoted to Venus, on the south side within the palace walls. The research, during which a part of the floor and a crypt were found, as well as architectural décor and parts of column bases and the coffered ceiling (fig. 14), confirmed this.[79] As well as these finds, a lion's paw suggests that this temple was dedicated to Cybele.[80] From the surrounding islands, the cult was known only in Brač.

---

[59] 1896, 87-89.
[60] Šašel Kos 1999, 82; In the article 'Matres Magnae in *SALONAE* – A Note', Šašel Kos provided the majority of relevant inscriptions from Dalmatia and Liburnia and from which it can be concluded that Magna Mater was, by far, much more respected then the rest of the deities present at that period.
[61] Medini 1981b, 191.
[62] Kuntić Makvić 2000, 117.
[63] Kubitschek 1896, 41-42; CIL III 14243; Graillot 1912, 493; Schillinger 1979, 64, 48; Medini 1981b, n°, 33; Vermaseren 1989, n° 158; Šašel Kos 1999, 83.
[64] Frankfurter 1884, 111, 28; CIL III 8675; Kubitschek 1896, 88; Drexler in Rocher, *Myth.Lex.* II, col. 2922; Waltzing 1899, 98, 296; Graillot 1912, 492-3; Dessau 1916, 4105; Vermaseren 1977a, 143; Schillinger 1979, 63f; Medini 1981b, n° 31; Medini 1985, 7, n° 3; Vermaseren 1989, n° 165; Šašel Kos 1999, 83.
[65] Medini 1981b, 191.
[66] CIL III 1953; Kubitschek 1896, 87; Drexler in Rocher, *Myth.Lex.* II, col. 2922; Graillot 1912, 492; Schillinger 1979, 62; Medini 1981b, n° 39; Vermaseren 1989, n° 157; Šašel Kos 1999. 83.
[67] BASD 11 (1888), 10, n° 5; CIL III 2676=9707; *BASD* 19 (1896), 88; Graillot 1912, 493, n. 1; Medini 1981b, n° 28.
[68] CIL III 1952=8567; Kubitschek 1896, 87; Drexler in Rocher, *Myth.Lex.* II, col. 2922; Graillot 1912, 492; Dessau 1916, 4106; Vermaseren 1977a, 142f; Schillinger 1979, 62, 42; Medini 1981b, n° 34; Vermaseren 1989, n° 166; Šašel Kos 1999. 83.
[69] Bulić 1923, 83-84; Zeiler 1929, 211, Schillinger 1979, 274, 688; Medini 1981b, n° 43; Medini 1985, 7-8, n° 5; Vermaseren 1989, n° 168; Šašel Kos 1999, 84.
[70] CIL III, 13903; BASD 1985, 3; Kubitschek 1896, 87; Drexler in Rocher, *Myth.Lex.* II, col. 2922; Hepding 1903, 189; Dölger 1922, 442; Graillot 1912, 493; Dessau, 1916, 4106; Vermaseren 1977a, 143; Schillinger 1979, 63, 42; Medini 1981b, n° 40; Vermaseren 1989, n° 167; Šašel Kos 1999, 83.
[71] Rendić Miočević 1953, 261; Medini 1981b, n° 35; Medini 1985, 7, n° 4; Vermaseren 1989, n° 155; Šašel Kos 1999, 83.
[72] Kuntić Makvić, 2000, 117.
[73] Medini 1981b, n° 36.
[74] BASD XI 1888, 177, n° 105; CIL III 8544=12814; BASD XVI 1893, 33, n° 13; Medini 1981b, n° 67.
[75] BASD XXI 1898, 141-144; CIL III 14674, Graillot 1912, 492; Medini 1981, n° 65; Vermaseren 1989, n° 153.
[76] 1981b, 186-188.
[77] BASD XVIII, 18; CIL III 13927; Graillot 1912, 491; Medini 1981b, n° 78.
[78] CIL III 2755; Medini 1981b, n° 79.
[79] Marasović 1968, 18; Medini 1981b, n° 50a; Marasović 1994.
[80] Medini 1981b, n° 50b.

The new cemetery in Škrip yielded an inscription (fig. 15) from which we know that there was a sanctuary dedicated to the Great Goddess and that Mescenia Tertulla, daughter of Publius, erected a portico with her own money.[81]

The cult was never deeply routed further from the coastal region nor in the purely autochthonic environments. While in some centres of the Roman provinces within the borders of the Republic of Croatia we follow a firm development, in other regions this cult was completely unknown. We find such examples in Narona and Epidaurus, Roman colonies where it would have certainly been expected for some traces of the cult to have occurred. *Pola* and *Nesactium* were cult centres in Histria, but the main centre of the region was Tergeste. We learn from the inscriptions that here was the office of an *archigallus*[82] and a Metroon[83] as well. The centre of the cult in Pannonia was Carnuntum confirmed by remarkable finds,[84] among which a tombstone that it is believed that belonged to a *gallus* or even to an *archigallus*.[85] The cult left deep traces in Aquincum, Poetovio, Brigetio and Emona. Onomastic researches showed the presence of Orientals in Pannonia.[86] Influential waves were coming from Thrace as well. So far, there is not any archaeological proof from the Pannonian centres within the borders of the Republic of Croatia that will direct us to any sacred cult buildings. It is however possible that there was a Metroon in *Mursa*.[87] A marble statue of Magna Mater[88] found in *Mursa* may have belonged to this supposed temple. *Siscia* has also yielded some important finds according to which we learn that Attis was especially known and worshipped.

Gradual decline of the Mother Goddess religion in the third, and its complete disappearance in the fourth century is a result of the general disapproval of polytheism and wholesale acceptance of Christianity in the provinces. As much as the rise of Christianity helped the collection of information about the cult of the Great Mother,[89] it also brought about the devastation of its monuments. The cult resisted the Christian attacks only in *Salona*, where it managed to be sustained all through the fourth century. We can find a reason for this in the fact that in the first centuries Christianity spread among members of the lower social levels, while the aristocracy, who better understood the philosophy of the cult as well as the eschatological and soteriological benefits expressed in the funeral monuments, were more inclined to the Goddess and her consort Attis.

The supporters and organisation of the Cult

The most important epigraphical record about the local organisation of the Mother Goddess cult comes from *Iader* and it stands as singular proof that there was an institution of the *archigallus* in the province of Dalmatia. Unfortunately, the inscription is lost and therefore it cannot be studied in detail. We know only of the transcript from CIL.[90] Lucius Barbunteius Demetrius is the only known *archigallus* from the territory of the Republic of Croatia. His service was in *Salona* (*archigallo salonitano*), while, it is believed, he died in *Iader* where this inscription was found. The tombstone was erected by his freedwoman Thallusa Calistera. This opens up the strong possibility that Barbunteius Demetrius did not have his own family and that he lived by the regulations of the Mother Goddess doctrine, if not as a eunuch, than certainly in celibacy.[91]

The interpretations of the other information from the inscription are different and contradictory. From the fifth column of the epitaph Graillot reads that this *archigallus* began his service at the age of 17 and that it lasted 58 years until his death at the age of 75.[92] An approximate chronological timeframe can be set if we have in mind the year 160 A.D. as the time limit when the emperor Antoninus Pius made his religious reforms. Assuming that Demetrius was appointed as *archigallus* immediately after the reforms we can determine the year of his birth (142/3) and his death (217/8). Vermaseren agreed with this hypothesis, although he believed that it is rather unusual for an *archigallus* to be given a lifelong service at such young age.[93] Suić, on the other hand, had a different opinion and considered the possibility that Demetrius was in service for seventeen years and was given this honour at the age of 58.[94] Medini accepted this explanation, but also offered arguments that are more reliable.[95] He pointed out that the name of the *archigallus* can also be used as another indicator of the time of his service. It was written with the *tria nomina* formula, which leads us to the middle of the second century when Demetrius performed service, and the beginning of the same century when he was born. This way of naming existed until the beginning of the second century when the prenomen disappeared from Roman onomastic formulas. If Demetrius was to be born in 142 or 143 A.D. as Graillot supposed, then his name would have probably had a different form in accordance with the loss of the prenomen. The other argument that supports the assumption that Demetrius became *archigallus* when he was 58 years of age is of linguistic nature and concerns the reading of the fifth column of the inscription. Because of the lack of the preposition *ab* in front of the form *annis*, which is an ablative of the plural of the noun *annus*, the translation is giving an answer to the question

---

[81] Gjurašin 1989, 17; Gjurašin 1990, 252.
[82] Vermaseren 1978, n° 241.
[83] Vermaseren 1978, n° 243.
[84] Vermaseren 1989, n° 93 – 107; Jobst 1998, 38.
[85] Vermaseren 1989, n° 97.
[86] Pinterović 1967, 68.
[87] Rendić-Miočević and Šegvić 1998, 11.
[88] Pinterović 1967b, 67-79; Selem 1980, n° 15; Vermaseren 1989, n° 124.
[89] By attacking the Mother Goddess cult, Christian philosophers described in their polemics in detail its 'brutal and barbaric' nature, which was important in terms of gathering valuable data about the ritual practices.

[90] CIL III 2920a.
[91] Graillot 1912, 231-232.
[92] 1912, 236, n.4.
[93] 1977a, 108.
[94] 1965b, 100.
[95] 1981a, 15-28.

'for how long'.⁹⁶ The service of the *archigallus* was connected with a temple, although not every temple had an *archigallus*. His engagement certainly goes in favour of the theses that a main temple existed in *Salona*. Barbunteius Demetrius was probably authorised for the neighbouring cult centres as well, where there was the service of sacerdotes.

The official form of the cult in *Senia*, *Aenona* and on the island of *Arba* was emphasised, as well as the one that was spreading with the Roman army, like the one in *Burnum* within the imperial cult. Yet, the organisation of the cult on the territory of the province of Dalmatia can be observed by another specific grouping of worshippers. We know of this distinctiveness in the province of Dalmatia from particular inscriptions on which the word *cognatio* is attested. In the Roman world the word *cognatio*⁹⁷ designates a certain blood relation and it is evidenced on eight Dalmatian inscriptions. Aside from the Salonitan, *cognatio* occurs on an inscription from Bijač,⁹⁸ as well as on one from *Burnum*.⁹⁹ A question arises about the time and the ground on which the Salonian *cognationes* were based. Rendić-Miočević and Alföldy are reconciled that the inscribed *cognatio* from *Burnum* represents a kind of a clan or a family in a broader sense. Alföldy also points out that *cognatio* is an institution typical for Liburnian society and is therefore based on the mother's line, while in *Salona* it had an exclusively religious character derived from the worshipped female divinity. Medini also believed that the Salonitan *cognationes* were gathered around a religious idea, even so the oldest documented one – *cognatio Clodiorum* was founded on basis of blood relation. In addition, this is the only *cognatio* which bears a name. At the same time, Medini followed the genesis of the community and concluded that by the time it was formed, it gravitated around Venus, and that Magna Mater became protectress in later times. This alternation coincides with the loss of the family basis while organising the communities.

All of the inscriptions that refer to cognationes are ex-votos and not necessarily in relation with the Great Mother. The term *cognatio* is never detected on funeral monuments,¹⁰⁰ which helps us conclude that the community did not have funerary character. One of the engagements of the *cognatio*, which we know of from one of the Salonitan inscriptions, was building sanctuaries in the Salonitan array and their renovation.¹⁰¹

The heterogeneity of the devotees points to the different spiritual needs that the Great Mother could have appeased. On one of these inscriptions, there is a record of a certain devotee named Ulpius Attalus (fig. 16).¹⁰² His name is of oriental origin; moreover, it is evident that it is a theophoric derivative of Cybele's consort Attis. Furthermore, Attalus's function is also written on the inscription – *collector cognationis*, which speaks of a certain organising of the members within the *cognatio*. This inscription is interesting from another aspect – the abbreviation VVBS followed by several explanations for its meaning.¹⁰³ Even the Great Mother was called *cognationis* (fig. 17),¹⁰⁴ a possessive genitive that has not been attested at any place where the Goddess was worshipped. It is a unique demonstration of a function of the Great Mother obtained in the *Salona* region.

On the inscription of P. Safinius Filucinus¹⁰⁵ who in the sanctuary of the Matres Magnae replaced the old altar with a new one, an affiliation from the mother's side is indicated, so we find out that his mother was the priestess Terentia (*Terentiae sacerdotis f(ilius)*). Medini points to the public character of the sanctuary were Filucinus was engaged and were his mother was in service. In this inscription there is also a notice of G. Clodius Gracilis, who was apparently a leading person in this *cognatio*, and most probably a member of the *gens Clodii* in *Salona*. According to this inscription, and plausibly to the one of Ulpius Attalus, we can conclude that Magna Mater was not the only goddess protectress of the *cognationes*. It is more likely that goddesses were alternating, or even that the members were vowed to other divinities. Polytheistic systems were opened complexes and within them different gods often fluctuated. For example, the hastiferi from Ostia, a college gathered around Ma-Bellona had also duties during the festivals of the Great Mother.¹⁰⁶ In this context, Šašel Kos mentions the case of the priest from Superaequum, who simultaneously performed duties towards Ceres, Venus, and the Mother of the Gods.¹⁰⁷

Judging by the number of proofs about the existence of the sanctuaries in this region, it is possible to draw the assumption that the *Salona* array was a certain *area sacra* to the members of the *cognationes*. Cybele, among her other capacities, was connected with thermal springs and

---

⁹⁶ If the form *annis* concerns the question 'since when', then the whole construction of the sentence would be *ab annis... usque ad...* According to the rules, this kind of a temporal ablative should be in singular (*ab anno*) which is not the case in this example; see Medini 1981a, 22.
⁹⁷ Medini studied this problem in detail (1985), but it was of interest to other scholars as well (Čače 1985, Kurilić 1995), according to whom *cognatio* was an expression designating the local affiliation from the fathers side.
⁹⁸ CIL III 9708.
⁹⁹ Rendić Miočević 1960, 165-168; Alföldy 1963, 81-87.
¹⁰⁰ Medini 1985, 8.
¹⁰¹ ...*de sua vota fanum ampliavit*. (VAHD XLVI 1923, 83-84; RA 1929, 211; Schillinger 1979, 274, 688; Medini 1981b, n° 43; Medini 1985, 7-8; Vermaseren 1989, n° 168; Šašel Kos 1999, 84).

¹⁰² It is important to notice that Graillot and Duthoy did not consider this inscription when dealing with the Mother Goddess cult monuments.
¹⁰³ The first interpretation was offered by Hula 1890, 99. According to him it is a vow to Venus and the abbreviation stands for *Veneri Victrici Bonae Sacrum*. Graillot agreed to this (Graillot 1912, 282). Another possible argument is that this abbreviation refers to *Viribus Valentibus Bonis Sacrum*, which associates the inscription to the genitals of the sacrificial bull (CIL III, 8676; Zeiller 1929, 210-11). The third plausibility is that the inscription is dedicated to the north italic deities *Vires* who personified corporeal strength (Medini 1981b, 8-11).
¹⁰⁴ Frankfurter 1884, 111, 28; CIL III, 8675; Kubitschek 1896, 88; Waltzing 1899, 98, 296; Drexler in Rocher, *Myth.Lex.* II, col. 2922; Graillot 1912, 492-3; Dessau 1916, 4105; Vermaseren 1977a, 143; Schillinger 1979, 63f; Medini 1981b, n° 31; Medini 1985, 7, n° 3; Vermaseren 1989, n° 165; Šašel Kos 1999, 83.
¹⁰⁵ Medini 1985, 17-18.
¹⁰⁶ Fishwick 1967, 145.
¹⁰⁷ 1999, 89.

holy curative rivers besides which her shrines were usually built.[108] In Dorylaeum, in Phrygia, the Goddess had an epithet Θερμηνή[109] which demonstrates that her iatric capabilities were in connection with thermal waters. The epithet σωτερία is also often found with the Goddess's name[110] and additionally speaks in favour of her healing and protective qualities. It can be supposed that the local population was aware of these powers of the Great Mother and that the river Iadro was another reason for gathering the *cognationes* and setting shrines devoted to the Goddess in this region. The soteriological aspects of the cult satisfied the needs of communities to protect the prosperity and welfare of its members. One of Cybele's divine duties was deflection of illnesses and misfortunes, while the iatric content of the cult is in complete compliance with the needs of the society, in this case, with a narrow community.

Cybele's soteriological role is often directed towards a group or a community. On an altar from Doghalar,[111] western Phrygia, we read an inscription dedicated to Μητρί θεῶν Ζινγοτηνῇ in order to protect the donor and his family, but also to protect the whole village out of which name (Ζίνγοτος) the Goddess's epithet derived. Cybele was also protectress of the Roman families, especially the Julio-Claudii. Moreover, she was protectress and Mother of the entire nation (*Mater patriae*). On this basis Livia was portrayed as the Great Mother.[112] By designating Cybele as protectress of communities, it is centred the positive opportunities during life, while the eschatological powers of Attis concern the after life. That is the reason why we often find the image of the young god on funeral monuments from the late antiquity.

The local existence of the college of *dendrophoroi* stands as another proof of the complexity of the Mother Goddess cult in these regions, as well an indication of the possible performance of the March festivals. One inscription from *Salona* bears the mention of *dendrophoroi*,[113] and there is also one from *Pola* (fig. 18).[114] From the latter monument, we find out that Laecanius Theodorus, a priest of the Great Mother (*sacerdos Matris Deorum Magnae Idaeae*) handed over a burial place to the *dendrophoroi* from *Pola* (*Dendrophoris Polensium*). The college of *dendrophoroi* existed also in the province of Pannonia, as proven by the inscription from *Siscia*.[115] In the wider region we find evidence of the existence of the college in Ljubljana.[116] The presence of this college draws attention to the possibility that the March festivals were performed in all three regions. The most numerous epigraphical finds with the mention of the *dendrophoroi* came from Ostia[117] and Rome,[118] but also from Campania[119] and Gaul.[120]

The emperor Claudius constituted the Roman college of dendrophoroi (or tree bearers) on his birthday[121] for the needs of certain rituals – the *dendrophorii* in the context of the March festivals (J. Lydus, *De mens.* 4, 59). The name of the college is a Latinized Greek compound (δένδρν + φέρο).[122] Their ritual duty was on the 22nd of March at the day of *Arbor intrat* when Attis's death was commemorated. *Dendrophoroi* also performed the ritual *taurobolium*.[123] The members were representatives of the middle class, and often included freedmen. Women could also be members, although they would have obtained only honorary functions.[124] Judging by their donations, which were often in gold, *dendrophoroi* often became wealthy. The college was abolished by a decree during the reign of Constantine.[125]

It is not certain whether this college existed only for ritual purposes or if it had an independent character based on a professional association of people involved in carpentry. It is more probable that they take their name exclusively from the duties within the festival cycle in March and that they were not connected at all with carpentry. It is known that associations were organized around the cult of the Great Mother, often of an exclusive and secret nature,[126] which is probably the case with the *dendrophoroi*.

The find from Bovillae[127] reveals an additional aspect of the college of *dendrophoroi*, which helps us comprehend its character even more. On this inscription from the time of the emperor Antoninus Pius the *dendrophoroi* are designated as *collegium salutare*. J. Carcopino believed that this denomination expresses the idea of salvation in the afterlife guaranteed by the Great Mother.[128] Sfameni Gasparro questioned this theory and considered whether this attribute could have referred to the obligation of the order in ensuring wellbeing and protection of the members during their lifetime.[129] On a contorniate medallion struck in honour of Faustina the Elder, where we recognise the *Phrygianum* on the Vatican, Cybele bears the epithet *salutaris*.[130] This was connected with the

---

[108] Graillot 1912b, 213-228; Sfameni Gasparro 1985, 86-7.
[109] Robert 1955, 78-82, Pl. XXI, 2.
[110] Sfameni Gasparro 1985, 88.
[111] Vermaseren 1977c, n° 121.
[112] Bieber 1969, 32-3.
[113] CIL III 8823; Waltzing 1899, 99, 302; Graillot 1912, 493; Марић 1933, 76; Schillinger 1979, 64, 48a; Medini 1981b, n° 41; Vermaseren 1989, n° 160.
[114] Kandler 1855, 251; CIL V, 481; Weisshäupl 1901, 202, n° 90; Sticotti 1914, 290, n. 3; Gnirs 1915, 75, n° 105; Dessau 1916, 4172; Swoboda 1969, 205, n° 16; Degrassi 1970, 625; Vermaseren 1978, n° 247; Girardi Jurkić 1999 II, 3.8.1.
[115] CIL III 10853; Kukuljević, 1873, 142; Graillot 1912, 487; Selem 1980, 201f, n°8; Tóth 1989, n°10.
[116] Swoboda 1969, 196, n°1.
[117] Vermaseren 1977c, n° 364, n° 386, n° 400, n° 408, n° 409, n° 412, n° 414.
[118] Vermaseren 1977c, n° 208, n° 212.
[119] Vermaseren 1978, n° 2, n° 4, n° 5, n° 13, n° 14,
[120] Vermaseren 1986, n° 314, n° 326, n° 342, n° 368, n° 372, n° 373, n° 374, n° 385, n° 389, n° 390, n° 391.
[121] CIL X 7; CIL VI 641; Fishwick, 1966, 201; Fishwick, 1967, 157.
[122] Fishwick, 1967, 147.
[123] Duthoy 1969, 94.
[124] Graillot 1912, 265; Thomas 1984, 1529.
[125] Thomas 1984, 1529.
[126] Sfameni Gasparro 1985, 69-73.
[127] Vermaseren 1977c, n° 464.
[128] 1926, 231-246.
[129] Sfameni Gasparro 1985, 102.
[130] Turcan 1996b, 51-2.

imperial recognition of this temple and the ritual that was performed in that location, which again emphasises the Goddess's soteriological aspects.[131]

---

[131] Sfameni Gasparro 1985, 88.

MYSTERY ASPECTS OF THE CULT

General characteristics

During the integration of Cybele and her paredros Attis, different elements of this cult were accepted and added in various mythological-ritual systems. They existed independently from each other, though simultaneously and inter-correlated, thus creating a rich and complex structure. The Mother Goddess cult adapted to many spiritual climates, but also to the personal needs of people, who, while performing the ritual practice, came into intimate contact with the divine couple. Besides the guarantee of fertility, a promise of personal salvation was offered to the worshippers that, apart from the conventionality of the official religion, led them to a completely different spiritual experience.

The definition set by R. Reitzenstein, according to which mystery cults are of secret, esoteric and initiating character, able to adapt within the flexible context of polytheism, is also applicable to the cult of the Mother Goddess. Mysteries represent a separate aspect of the general cult of a specific deity, when, through the experience of the sacred, one can reach a change of consciousness.[132] Burkert also adds that the initiation rituals are of voluntary, personal and secret character and that their primary goal is the alternation of consciousness through the experience of sacredness.[133]

Initiation is a key word when defining the mystery cults. However, what separates the mystery initiations from initiation in general is the inner change of the initiated,[134] as opposed to his social change. Another important feature of mystery initiation is the possibility of rebirth. In the context of mystery cults, initiation can be understood as death and birth in a spiritual sense, during which a change of consciousness prevails. The initiated is reborn in the world of new perception, knowledge and light; he crosses from one ontological level to another. Therefore, the term *rite of passage* is often used while describing mystery initiation rituals. U. Bianchi[135] very schematically explains the levels crossed during initiation – separation, marginalisation, and finally aggregation, when the initiated becomes part of the group.

The practice of mystery rituals is a direct experience as opposed to dogma, and is often described as 'seeing the light'. The initiated experiences the realm of death and saw the divine light which transformed him. But death is a secret, and secrecy is another defining characteristic of mystery cults.[136] Pausanius (7, 17, 9) speaks of the divine nature of Attis in which the secret (ἀπόρρητον) is contained. There is no mention of theological books within the realm of the Mother Goddess cult. The worshippers were relying on myth or on the *hieros logos*, to be more precise, transmitted by secret ritual. Secrecy was a duty of the members of mystery communities; those who belonged and were initiated to the mysteries were separated from 'the others'. The community propagated faith, but did not reveal the essence of the epiphany; secrecy was the foremost attracting force of the mysteries.[137]

In general, the organisation of the mystery religions had three different, but compatible forms; it can be recognised in the practice of the itinerants or charismatics, in the organised clergy linked to a certain sanctuary, or in the grouping of worshippers in religious, independent, and exclusive associations.[138] The mysteries of Cybele were of oriental character and, unlike the Greek ones, not strictly related to shrines and cult places, but rather spread and attached to other mythological and ritual systems.[139] In order to continue with further interpretations of the characteristics of the Mother Goddess cult which are of interest in this part of the work, it is necessary, above all, to distinguish variant forms of the cult, bearing in mind the typological difference between 'the mystery' and 'the mystic'.[140]

Furthermore, mystery cults are formed around gods with certain common characteristics, in that way creating a separate category within the polytheistic pantheon. Starting from the division made by Plutarch of the divine beings as gods and demons (*De Iside*, 25), U. Bianchi continues to describe the evolution of the mystery gods.[141] The nature of demons is mutable and reflects the change of the nature cycles, while their mythology describes the sufferings and death that they go through in order to realize the alteration and become mystery gods. The vegetative character some of them contain is a key element while explaining the so-called near eastern 'fertility rites', during which the divine vicissitude was invoked as a guarantee for the fertility of the earth, but also as hope for the continuity of life. Being transformed further through their evolution, demons pass from the

---

[132] Reitzenstein 1978, 111-169; This preliminary defininition was accepted by other scholars, see Cumont 1914; Bianchi 1976; Burkert 1987; Sfameni Gasparro 1985.
[133] 1987, 11
[134] Burkert 1987, 8.
[135] 1976, 3-4.
[136] Burkert 1987, 9, 74.

[137] Burkert 1987, 45-46.
[138] Burkert 1987, 30-32.
[139] Sfameni Gasparro, 1985, xiii.
[140] Regarding this difference, there is also the explanation offered by Sfameni Gasparro: '...if the term mystery defines a mythical – ritual complex of the Eleusis type, in the organic interaction of all its aspects, precedence is given in this definition to the ritual component, with initiation and esotericism, practised within a sanctuary, by a specialised body of priests... The term 'mystic' can then be used to define those cults which, both inside and outside the Greek world, do not necessarily present an esoteric – initiatory structure but are centred round a superhuman figure with characteristics which are substantially analogous to the god of the mysteries and (/or) tend to give rise to a type of relationship between man and deity similar to the one established in the 'mystery'. Here, in fact, the nature of the god and the situation of man appear to be intimately connected in a special relationship, so that the condition of the worshipper is defined in virtue of his participation in a cult which celebrates the vicissitude of the deity...' (Sfameni Gasparro 1985, 6-7.).
[141] 1976, 2.

level of mystic gods onto a higher level – they become mystery gods. Mystery gods are, therefore, those subject to change. The rituality that they required was not particularly changed, although it gained an initiatory-esoteric character that allowed more personal relationship with the 'divine'. In the Hellenistic-Roman period these oriental rituals grew to be public cults, but still they preserved their mystery character within the communities developed around them.[142]

The spiritual structure of Cybele, although going through an intensive process of Hellenisation, kept some genuine, Neolithic elements, such as a relationship with the agrarian rhythms, music, and mountains. Cybele is the Mother Earth with distinctive chthonic connotations and exactly because of this primary concept she was accepted and completely integrated within the Greek religion. The cult in classical Greece was characterised with the mystic aspect reflected through its orgiastic character, hence positioned closer to the Dionysian ritual circle.[143] The nocturnal ceremonies devoted to Cybele were performed high in the mountains and in rustic surroundings; connected to agrarian rhythms, they assured the fertility of crops and the renewal of vegetation. Usually she was celebrated by women, who, following the frenetic sound of tympana and cymbals, the holy instruments of the Goddess, reached states of ecstasy. *Mania*, a condition inflected and removed by the Goddess herself, led her followers into orgiastic and spiritual catharsis. In the terminology of the Dionysian ceremonies, the one accepting the spirit of the god was called βάκχος. By analogy, in the rites of Cybele, the adepts came in contact with the 'divine' through ecstatic dances and were called κύβεβος, as someone possessed by Cybele.[144]

Besides the typical enthusiastic-orgiastic form of the cult of the classical period, Cybele was later identified with the Greek mystery cults concerning other aspects. In the Hellenistic period, the mystic character of the Goddess gained an initiatory-esoteric dimension that lifted her cult to the level of mysteries of the Eleusinian model.[145] As opposed to the previous form of the religious practice, which was objective and collective, it now developed a more subjective and individual character. There are indications that the cult of Cybele had contained some mystery elements from its early times in Asia Minor. On a decree of the Persian governor from Sardis there is a mention of mysteries devoted to Agdistis, Sabazius, and Ma, ceremonies that did not allow the presence of the priests of Zeus. L. Robert[146] believes that this inscription bears the first mention of mysteries related to the Great Mother from the region of Asia Minor and that it dates from the fourth century B.C., the time of Artaxerxes II Mnemon. On the other hand, Vermaseren dated this monument to the second century A.D.[147] Judging by other inscriptions, the cult in Asia Minor certainly developed its mystery form by the beginning of the Roman imperial period, but nothing is known of the rituals or of its ideological background.[148] Therefore, it is much safer to say that the mystery form of the cult, or its initiatory-esoteric form, developed in the Hellenistic period as a result of the direct influence of Eleusis. We recognise the institutional form of the mysteries created around the figure of Cybele, although we cannot speak of the eschatological benefits offered to the worshippers during practice. Thracian mysteries of the Kabiri also acted upon the development of the mysteries of Cybele. Marazov draws attention to the closeness of the Eleusinian mysteries and the ones of the Kabiri. He points out the possibility that the roots of both these cults can be traced in the pre-Hellenic period and that the Thracians might have been their founders.[149]

The mystic development of the cult traced through the image of Attis as a reflection of the natural powers that die and are born again, as well as his Phrygian origin, are foundations that place this god as a carrier of the oriental mystic aspect. He is part of the entirety of the near eastern rituals that evoke the divine vicissitude, recognising the nature cycle of vegetation.[150] We recognise the etiology of the myth of Attis in the ritual practice of the *galloi* from Pessinunt where they embody the god and relive his destiny through self castration (*imitatio dei*).[151] The form of the cult that developed in Piraeus had some recognisable Phrygian elements. Here, a private association gravitated around the figures of Cybele and Attis. Although we cannot reconstruct the *Attideia*, we know of the ritual of preparing two thrones that leads us toward the local existence of mystery rituals. It is possible that they celebrated the death and the resurrection of Attis, two separate ceremonies that required this kind of preparation. In any case, we are left with the fact that in Piraeus, besides the Mother of Gods, Attis was worshipped as a reflection of the mystery aspect of the Phrygian religious system.[152]

The Phrygian elements of the cult were especially expressed in the Roman festivals in March honouring Attis. While Cybele was the one enabling eschatological benefits, the model of the ritual practice was created upon the figure of Attis. The interpretation of Attis's mystic aspect in the March ceremonies is contained in the recognition of the ancient element of divine vicissitude as a paradigm of the death and rebirth of natural forces. It can be said that the main determination of these public rites is the ritual death that led the initiates to higher states of consciousness. Passing through 'death', the initiate passed the way of the god and in that manner understood how to reach the offered higher consciousness. All these elements allow the underlining

---

[142] Reitzenstein 1978, 13-14.
[143] Sfameni Gasparro 1985, 23.
[144] Sfameni Gasparro 1985, 15.
[145] Sfameni Gasparro 1985, 8-25.
[146] 1975, 306-330.
[147] 1987, 456.
[148] Sfameni Gasparro 1985, 64-73.
[149] Маразов 1992, 139.
[150] Bianchi and his student rejected the categorization of the so-called 'vegetation gods' made by Frazer and replaced it with 'dèi in vicenda' (Bianchi 1979, 12f). This generalization was further criticized by Burkert (1987, 76).
[151] Burkert 1987, 77.
[152] Hepding 1903, 136-138; Sfameni Gasparro 1985, 50.

of the mystic character of the Mother Goddess cult in Roman imperial times.[153] *Dies sanguinem* was the high point of the mourning period and the last day of fasting. The *galloi* would dance ecstatically around the holy pine tree, following the sounds of cymbals and flutes, flagellating themselves, while their blood dripped on the pine tree and on the altars in the temple. The ritual culminated with their emasculation.[154] The rituals on the night before the festivity and joy called *pannychis* or *mesonyctum* is known.[155] On this same night, the holy pine tree was buried, a ritual which, according to the words of Macrobius (*Sat.* 1, 21, 10), symbolically determined katabasis, or descent within the sphere of the Underworld. The pine tree was buried as a reminder of the mythological burial of Attis in Pessinunt. Damascius (*Vit.* 1.131) speaks of this ritual as a deliverance from death in the Mother Goddess festivals.

Attis is the one who, in this case, transmitted the vision of the cosmic existence of the soul and contained the eschatological principal of the cult. The destiny of the soul follows the destiny of the god, who has the role of mediator; he descends into matter and returns on a divine level. Hippolytus[156] and the Gnostic sect of the Naassenes saw Attis in exactly this manner. According to them, he is the divine intermediary principle that offers the example of liberating the soul through castration.[157] Neo-Platonists explained the Phrygian myth in the similar way. In the mysteriosophic interpretation of the myth, Julian the Apostate[158] postulated the initiation of the *galloi* as a guarantee of life beyond life. Sallustius (*De diis et mundo*, 4) adds that after initiation, milk was drunk as an allusion of rebirth.

Sfameni Gasparro penetrates very deeply in explaining the soteriological aspects of the mystery cults from a modern perspective, perceiving this phenomenon through the prism of the Mother Goddess spiritual system, in which she sees a *flexible complex of guarantees provided by participation in this cult*.[159] Soteriological aspects are a key part of the cult, recognisable in the early period of its formation. Cybele is the protectress of well-being and has the power of medical healing. The cult of Cybele appeared in Greece, as in Rome, after great wars. The Persian Wars and the Punic Wars were among the most dreadful in antiquity. Horrible and destructive powers of death called upon the Great Mother, the Saviour. Her soteriological character is now very well defined on the national level, and does not affect the individual but the whole nation. But the main saviour idea presented in the cult in Roman times is the ritual evoking of Attis's destiny.[160] The soteriological moments in the festivals in March are manifested in the joy during which the resurrection of Attis was celebrated, hence the resurrection of men. Therefore in the scriptures of the Damascius (*Vita Isidori*, cod. 242, 345a), the celebration of the *Hilaria* is considered as an opportunity for salvation from Hades.

Yet another ritual of the Great Mother carried dominant mystery and soteriological aspects that were necessary for pious people of later antiquity. *Taurobolium*, an exclusively Roman creation within the frame of the cult, was first held as beneficiary for the cultic community, although also honouring the emperor. It became an initiatory ritual of the Roman aristocracy,[161] whose members, through the blood of the killed bull, gained a guarantee of well-being over the next twenty years, as well as the possibility of regeneration. Later, the *taurobolium* developed clear soteriological values projected in an eschatological dimension.[162] On one inscription from the second half of the fourth century we read that the initiated were *in aeternum renatus*,[163] an idea that, in this context, might have occurred through the influence of Christianity. The ritual of *taurobolium* is compared with Christian baptism; moreover, a possible developmental line can be detected moving from paganism to Christianity, where bulls' blood was replaced with water.[164]

Discussions about common elements of Christian and mystery cults occur quite frequently,[165] although the differences between these two systems are immanent and radical.[166] Similarities, on the other hand, between Christianity and the Mother Goddess religion, especially bearing in mind mystery aspects, are strongly present. A. T. Fear[167] underlines some of them, based mainly on soteriological and eschatological moments, considering at the same time the reasons why the cult religion in late antiquity evolved into a system with similar spiritual concepts as Christianity. Some eschatological and soteriological concepts of the cult developed later in accordance with the late antique religious trends. The author mentions the possibilities of intentional changing of the religion in order to create an opposing system to Christian religion. In the fifth century there was even a doctrinal writing of the theology of the cult, a work of the Neo-Platonist Proclus.[168] This change was in fact a result of the fierce attacks of Christian apologetics.[169]

---

[153] Sfameni Gasparro 1985, 63.
[154] Turcan 1996b, 45.
[155] Vermaseren 1977a, 115-6.
[156] *Ref.* 5, 6-11; Hepding 1903, 33ff.
[157] See also Lancellotti 2002, 119-125.
[158] *Orat.* 5, 159-180: Hepding 1903, 51ff.
[159] 1985, 104.
[160] Sfameni Gasparro 1985, 125.

[161] Reitzenstein 1987, 22.
[162] Sfameni Gasparro 1983, 199-232; Sfameni Gasparro 1985, 118.
[163] Sextilius Agesilaus Aedesius 376 AD (CIL VI, 510).
[164] Fear 1996, 40.
[165] More about transmission of element of mystery religion in Christian sacraments see Nock 1952, 177-213.
[166] Burkert 1987, 3.
[167] 1996, 37-50.
[168] The work was lost, but we know of it from the biography of Proclus, written by his successor Martin (*Vit. Procli* 33).
[169] Fear 1996, 44.

Mystery aspects of the Cult on the material from the Republic of Croatia

The atmosphere into which the Mother Goddess cult developed in the region of Illyricum reflected a general acceptance of the eastern cults with mystery connotations. The Egyptian cults of Isis and Serapis,[170] as well as Mythraism[171] coexisted in these parts of the Empire. The presence of Sabazius[172] is another strong indication that directly refers to the existence of the mysteries of Cybele, specifically their eastern form.[173] In order to continue with the enquiry of the mystery character of the cult, we shall consider several features of the Croatian cult monuments. It is rather difficult to recognize the mystery aspects of the cult in the provinces. The mystery substrate can predominantly be found in the iconographical symbolism that became universally standardized by the spread of Roman religious trends, but also in the votive inscriptions that directly expose the spiritual impulses and practices of individuals.[174] Besides the iconographical interpretation which will follow, we can broaden our knowledge of the mystery aspects of the local Mother Goddess cult by examining the personal vows.

Oriental religions which had developed mystery aspects spread towards the West, mainly owing to their soteriological characteristics. Divine protection and the assurance of eternal salvation were religious experiences offered to worshippers,[175] enhancing them to make personal vows to the Great Mother. Votive religion, according to Burkert,[176] forms the background of the practice of the mysteries because it itself is a form of personal religion. Personal and direct experience is the element that connects mysteries and votive religion. We find vows to the Goddess in several examples on the Salonitan inscriptions. The worshippers built sanctuaries or rebuilt and renewed earlier ones. The votive character can be recognized on other Croatian finds as well, like on the smaller statues of Cybele from *Salona*, or on the appliqués with Attis's bust from *Aenona* and its surroundings.

Curia Prisca renewed the sanctuary, performed the sacrificial ritual, erected statues of domestic gods, and donated accessories: *tympana, cymbala, catillum* and *forfices*.[177] *Tympana* as well as *cymbala* are typical liturgical objects of the Mother Goddess cult. Apart from being used during the ecstatic dances and the megalensian pompa, they also had a symbolic meaning in mystery rituals. The well known mystery formulas of Clement of Alexandria,[178] and the later one of Firmicus Maternos,[179] speak of these instruments as crucial in the performance of Roman initiation rituals. It is not precisely clear what these Christian polemics described, but it is certain that *tympana* and *cymbala* had symbolic meaning during rituals.[180] The writings of the Christian apologetics are often considered in the attempts to reconstruct the Roman Mother Goddess mystery rituals, according to which it was exactly through these holy instruments that one could reach the religious secret. Besides *tympana* and *cymbala*, in this inscription there is a mention of *catillum*, a religious bowl, and *forfices* as well. So far, there are no known depictions of this kind of object in iconography, nor is there a mention of it in relation to ritual. Scissors are a practical object, without any particular symbolic meaning within the cult, at least not known to us. *Forfices*, on the other hand, can also signify an instrument similar to contemporary forceps and it can be presupposed that it was used as a kind of a gripper during the religious devirilisation of the sacrificial victim.

The existence of an organized clergy of which the *galloi* were the representatives can also stand as an indicator of practising the mysteries in these regions. The direct connection between the *galloi* and the mysteries is particularly apparent during the festivals in March, and especially accentuated in the documents of later antiquity.[181] Minutius Felix (*Oct.* 22, 1-4) clearly places the Phrygian myth and the ritual of the *galloi* in the category of mystery cults. Nevertheless, the organisation of *cognationes* in the *Salona* array leads us even more towards the possible local practice of mysteries. It is very likely that these organisations were of secret and exclusive character and that the members practised the mysteries of Cybele. It is well known that the mystery element was above all maintained within the private associations that developed around the cult.[182] Several examples direct us to the possibility that the *cognationes* organised around the sanctuaries of the Great Mother were familiar with the esoteric-initiatory form of the cult. Although, the cult of Cybele in Greece contained mainly mystic aspects, we also follow the institutionalised forms of the mysteries; the *orgeones* from Piraeus practised the Phrygian mystery rites. On an inscription from Argos we read about a community of the initiates (κοινὸν τῶν μυστῶν) in relation to the Great Mother.[183] We also know of a community of initiates in Pessinunt from the first century whose members were called Ἀτταβοκαοί.[184] The esoteric-initiatory structure is also found in the *thiasus* near Juvadjà where the mysteries were practised in the

---

[170] Selem 1972.
[171] Miletić 1996.
[172] Medini 1980.
[173] Sfameni Gasparro 1985, 67.
[174] Burkert 1987, 12ff.
[175] Reitzenstein 1978, 17.
[176] Burkert 1987, 12.
[177] CIL III 1952=8567; Kubitschek 1896, 87; Drexler in Rocher, *Myth.Lex.* II, col. 2922; Graillot 1912, 492; Dessau 1916, 4106; Vermaseren 1977a, 142f; Schillinger 1979, 62, 42; Medini 1981b, n°34; Vermaseren 1989, n°166; Šašel Kos 1999, 83.

[178] (*Protreptikos* 2,15,3) ἐκ τυμπάνου ἔφαγον· ἐκ κυμβάλου ἔπιον· ἐκερνοφόρησα· ὑπὸ τὸν παστὸν ὑπέδυν.
[179] (*De errore profanorum religionum*, 18,1) *de tympano manducavi, de cymbalo bibi et religionis secreta perdidici quod graeco sermone dicitur* - ἐκ τυμπάνου βέβρωκα, ἐκ κυμβάλου πέπωκα, γέγονα μύστης Ἄττεως.
[180] Turcan 1996, 53.
[181] Sfameni Gasparro 1985, 76-77; Lancellotti 2002, 109-110.
[182] Reitzenstein 1978, 13-14.
[183] Vermaseren 1982, n° 469; Sfameni Gasparro 1985, 21.
[184] Hepding 1903, 79; Sfameni Gasparro 1985, 70.

caves used as sanctuaries to the Goddess.[185] In Rome, organised *collegia* had their role in the performances of the mystery rites during March festivals. The *dendrophoroi* were one of them. Medini draws an analogy with the *dendrophoroi* when he refers to the Salonitan *cognationes*.[186] The *cognationes* in the *Salona* array organised around the Great Mother were based upon the soteriological and the eschatological aspects of the cult, and therefore closely related to its mystery character.

Mysteries are predominantly of initiatory character, while the *taurobolium* was one of the main initiatory rituals within the Mother Goddess religion in later antiquity. This perspective on the comprehension of the mystery aspects of the ritual can be used for the analysis of some of the finds from the Republic of Croatia. However, the question whether the practice of *taurobolia* was performed in this region remains open. Medini sees the monument from *Asseria* (fig. 19) as an indisputable indicator of criobolia.[187] This *ara crioboliata* is incorporated in the corpus of taurobolic monuments compiled by Duthoy. It depicts a male figure in relief, holding a *cornucopia* in his left hand, while in his right there is a rectangular object which is generally considered as an ascium.[188] On the right side of the monument there is a relief depiction of a jug, a ram's head below it, and a knife on the right. This monument was dedicated to the Great Mother by Petronius Philippus and it was found together with a sacrificial altar honouring *Ianus Deus Pater*.[189] It is possible that these deities were worshipped together, in which case this would be a unique example of a form of religious union.

Perhaps the ritual of *taurobolium* was performed in *Iader* as well. The find on which Suić relies when he assumes that this ritual was known in this part of the Empire is a square pool found on the Zadar Forum (figs. 20, 21).[190] This pool is positioned besides the left staircase of the Forum, in front of the frontal wall of the Capitolium. The entire stone floor together with the pool is lower than the level of the pavement by 10 cm. The pool has a well-defined frame with a 4 cm deep and 5 cm wide groove. The average width of the enclosed pit is 0.60 m while its depth is almost 2 m. Suić believes that it is a *fossa sanguinis* and that the blood of the sacrificed animal flowed down the drain and into the pool. Suić also places the image of a Medusa on the balustrade of the Capitolium in the same context and explains that it would have contributed to the entire atmosphere of the taurobolic ritual. He also considers that the ivory box found in Zadar, now part of the collection of the Archaeological museum, supposedly illustrates the taurobolic ritual. It is 10 cm high and 17.5 cm long and dated to the third century. On one side of the box there are two Amors leading a bull, while on the other side and on the lid is a divinisation on which Suić based his claim that the *taurobolium* had a public character. Duthoy, on the other hand, disproves this theory pointing to the incomplete argumentation that could connect the supposed *fossa sanguinis* and the ivory box. He refers to the description given by Prudentius that it is not compatible with the situation found on the Forum in Zadar; the pit into which the initiate would be placed in order for the bloody ritual to be performed had to be significantly deeper.[191] However, we can assume that a blood sacrifice was performed in the Forum, but there is no concrete evidence that leads us towards the conclusion that it was in honour of the Great Mother.

During the attempt to isolate the initiatory form of the cult another find from Zadar attracts our attention. It is an underground chamber with frescoes with clear mystery connotations. We will say more about the fresco when we consider the iconography of the local cult, while on this occasion we will keep our attention on the chamber itself. It was part of a complex of other Roman buildings from the second century placed 70 m southwest of the Forum, among which were a cistern and a room with mosaic floor. The building has small dimensions – 5.20 m long, 3.45 m wide, while the walls are 2 m high on average. In comparison with the others, this building is significantly lower and is considered to be below ground level. A fragmented marble plate (fig. 22) which reveals the name of Magna Mater was found inside the chamber and proves that this building was dedicated to the Goddess.[192] By the beginning of the third century the situation with these buildings was altered in order for a Severan basilica to be built by the porch on the southeast side of the Forum.[193] Therefore, the building in question was no longer in use.

Underground chambers were used while performing the rituals of the cult. Nicander,[194] when writing about the mysteries in honour of the Great Mother and Attis, mentions the holy underground places (θαλάμαι) devoted to the Goddess. Underground rooms related to the mystery form of the cult allude to *katabasis*, or ritual descent into the Underworld. This initiatory ritual is typical of the Mother Goddess cult, but also of other mystery cults with whom the Great Mother came into contact. It was performed in Eleusis as an allusion to the pursuit of Persephone.[195] During the initiations of the Thracian Bendis, another goddess close to Cybele, this ritual was also practised.[196] Nevertheless, within the context of the Mother Goddess cult as it was known in the territory of Illyricum, it would be more noteworthy to consider the cult of the Kabiri, where the ritual of *katabasis* was also evidenced. The cult spread through

---

[185] Waldmann 1978, 1309-1315; Sfameni Gasparro 1985, 71.
[186] Medini 1985, 38.
[187] Medini 1981b, 227, 398.
[188] CIL III, 9935; Duthoy 1969, 13, n° 7.
[189] Medini 1981b, 229.
[190] Suić 1965b, 109-114.
[191] Duthoy 1968, 622-629.
[192] Suić 1965b, 100-101.
[193] Suić 1965b, 119-122; The author supposed that the sanctuary was moved to a different building, but we do not have any archaeological evidence. For the relocation of the Metroon in Nicomedia and the possibility of a similar situation in *IADER* see Kuntić – Makvić 2000.
[194] *Alexipharm* 6-8.
[195] Cosmopoulos 2003, 263.
[196] Маразов 1994, 57-68.

Asia Minor, northern Greece, and on the Thracian islands of the Aegean Sea.[197] The Kabiri were often identified with the Great Gods of Samothrace,[198] among which the Great Goddess Cybele can be recognized.[199] There is an interesting mythological relationship of the two important centres of the cult of the Kabiri, Samothrace and Thebes, with the Adriatic coast. Diodorus Siculus (5.48.4 – 50.1) wrote about Kadmos being initiated on Samothrace. There he married Harmonia in a wedding ceremony organised by the gods, during which rituals of the Great Mother were performed.[200] Kadmos, after he founded Thebes, came to the land of the Illyrians and ruled the Enheleans (19.53.3-5). Much was written about the coming of the mythological couple to Illyricum,[201] where, according to the legend, they were transformed into snakes, died and were buried. Another mythological affiliation of the Adriatic with the cult of the Great Mother is the legend of the Argonauts, a metaphor of the ancient road that connected the Black Sea with the region of the north Adriatic See. We read in Appolonius of Rhodes (4, 330) of the return of the Argonauts and their journey through the Danube to the Adriatic Sea. There is a mention of two Brigian Islands and a local temple dedicated to Artemis. The islands were named after the Briges, peoples from the Balkans who were equated in antiquity with the Phrygians,[202] the main bearers of the cult of Cybele.

In principal, one can gather more information about the mystery cults from the iconography of the cult than from the epigraphical evidence; above all their language consists of symbols and allegories.

---

[197] Маразов 1994, 81.
[198] Hemberg 1950, 11-12, 27-28, 318-25; Cole 1984, 3.
[199] Cole 1984, 3; Welch 1996, 467-473, Tab. 89-92.
[200] See also Clinton 2003, 67-8.
[201] For more on this mythological subject see Šašel Kos 1993; Kuntić Makvić 1994; Katičić 1995.
[202] For the Briges see Петрова 1996.

ICONOGRAPHY

Cybele

Only a few Roman statues of Magna Mater from the provinces survived antiquity; they are usually found fragmented or decapitated. We find the same situation with Croatian finds. Cybele on Croatian monuments can be seen in fully sculpted and in the usual canonised 'Agorakritos' style,[203] the one most often found in Roman provinces. However, among Croatian statues there are some truly unique examples. Of all Croatian monuments with the image of Cybele, the fresco from *Iader*, which at the same time is the only painted depiction of a ritual in this region, gives us the most information of the way the Mother Goddess cult was celebrated in Dalmatia. Besides the image of the Goddess, this fresco contains other figures and motifs of mystery character. Therefore, it will be elaborated separately. Goddess iconography on the Pannonian finds also reveals elements of the Mother Goddess mystery rituality and greatly contributes in creating the general picture of the cult.

The most representative statues of the Goddess from the Republic of Croatia are certainly the ones from *Senia*. Medini, their production dating from the late first, or middle of the second century,[204] while Cambi, based on the technical characteristics, moved the dating one century later.[205] Judging by their dimensions and craftsmanship, these statues were most likely furnishing the local temple dedicated to the Great Mother. One of these, found in three fragments and referred to as statue A (fig. 23),[206] represents the Goddess seated, as usual, on a high-backed throne. She is dressed in a *chiton* and a long *himation* and wears sandals on her feet. Two lions flank her body, the left one completely destroyed. Statue B (fig. 24)[207] differs from the previous one in many ways. The Goddess is once again seated, not on a throne but a rock. The sides of this statue are decorated with different animals. On the right there is a bull, a sheep below him, and a lion's head. On the left we see another bull and a head of a goat with large horns. We assume that there was a lion on this side as well, but due to the damage it is difficult to say. All these animals are typical of the Goddess's iconography. Her aspects of Mother Goddess and Mistress of Animals are emphasized. While the first statue is an example of a typical way of showing Cybele, the other one does not have any adequate analogies.[208] The statues are imported, most probably from Asia Minor.[209] A marble head found in *Senia* (figs. 25, 26) also attracts attention as a possible Cybele.[210] It has been affirmed that this head did not belong to the already mentioned statues even if it is from the same period.[211] The hair is braided in *crobylos*, which is often seen among the maternal goddesses and beginning in the Hellenistic period. Cybele's hair was treated in the same fashion as, for example, on the head from Samothrace (fig. 27).[212]

Salona, so far, has yielded seven marble statues of the Goddess, all of them much damaged, probably from the time of the acceptance of the Christianity, when the monuments of the pagan religions were being destroyed. She is crowned and seated on a throne in the company of her loyal lions. These statues are of smaller dimensions which point to their votive character (figs. 28-33). The only specificity is the *cista mystica* as an additional attribute on two of the Salonitan statues (figs. 28, 29).[213] *Cista mystica* is a typical ritual object into which *hierà* was held. It was used in the mystery rites and it can be seen on the Mother Goddess monuments as a reminder of the esoteric aspect of the Phrygian cult.[214] However, *cista mystica* is not a usual attribute of the Goddess. It can be seen as an attribute of the *galloi*, as seen on the lid of the sarcophagus of the *archigallus* from Ostia (fig. 34),[215] in the niche of the relief from Lanuvium (fig. 35),[216] where it is depicted together with the rest of the objects typical of this cult, but never in the hands of the Goddess. In this context, we might even consider the ivory box from Zadar, with a depiction of two Amors leading a sacrificial bull,[217] which could have served as an instrument in the Mother Goddess mystery rites.

The Salonitan statues can clearly be evaluated as provincial fabrication that leads us to a justified claim that there was an art workshop in *Salona*, from where all the statues found in the city came. By comparing these statues with the ones from *Senia*, significant differences can be noticed. The Senian ones are made in white marble and are work of better craftsmanship. They are, without doubt, imported, bearing in mind the inferior status of this town compared to *Salona*. Namely, *Salona* had the conditions for its own production. There are,

---

[203] The Cybele statue of Agorakritos from the renewed Metroon on the Athenian Agora was by far her most famous sculpture in antique times. Unfortunately, it was never found, but it is believed that it served as a model for other artists who represented Cybele's figure. After Arian's description (*Peripl.* 9) from the second century, she was depicted as a mature woman, sitting with dignity on her throne and holding a tympanum. She is accompanied by her loyal lions that additionally emphasize her power.
[204] Medini 1981b, n° 5, 6.
[205] Cambi 1993, 41.
[206] SZ 3 (1967-8), 20; Medini 1978, 737–739, pl. 149–151; Medini 1981b, n° 5; Vermaseren 1989, n° 129; Cambi 2005b, 123, fig. 184.
[207] SZ 3 (1967-8), 20; Degmedžić 1952, 252-4; Glavičić 1968, 20f; Medini 1978, 734–736, pl. 143, 147; Medini 1981b, n° 4; Vermaseren 1989, n° 130; Cambi 2005b, 123-124, fig. 185.

[208] Cambi (2005b, 36) considers the statue from Corinth (Vermaseren 1982, n° 459) that represents Cybele seated on the rock. The attributes on this statue are, however, different from the one from *Senia* and do not completely agree with the character of the Goddess to be shown. Therefore, we can not speak of an adequate analogy.
[209] Cambi 1993, 42.
[210] Degmedić 1952, 254, fig. 4; Medini 1978, 736, n.11, pl. 148, 1; Medini 1981b, n° 6.
[211] Cambi (2005b, 35). The author points to the possibility that the head might have belonged to an Artemis of an Aphrodite statue.
[212] Welch 1996, 468.
[213] Medini 1981b, n° 45, 46.
[214] Sfameni Gasparro 1985, 75.
[215] Vermaseren 1977c, n° 446.
[216] Vermaseren 1977c, n° 466.
[217] Suić 1965b, 109-112.

however, variations in the treatment of the Salonitan statues, though with less differences in the details, such as the height of the back of the throne. The statue from *Epetium*[218] is again of standard form and has a votive character judging by its small dimensions. It is dated to the second or third century at the latest. The Goddess is on a throne, dressed in *chiton* and *himation*. There are traces of lion figures visible on the damaged sides of the throne.

Cybele, together with Attis, is depicted only on the relief from *Burnum*.[219] Iconographical affiliations with other deities on the Croatian monuments cannot be determined with certainty. Only one monument directs us to this possibility – the marble slab on the old bell-tower from the cathedral in Split (fig. 36).[220] Together in a composition with Hercules, Minerva, Jupiter, Juno and Mars, there is a depiction of a female deity with a long sceptre and a crown representing the walls of a city (fig. 37). The goddesses identifiable in this figure can be narrowed down to two – *Tyche Salonitana* and Cybele. Cambi, as opposed to Abramić, believes that besides the special crown, the sceptre, an attribute that is not typical for Tyche, certifies that this is a depiction of Cybele after all. This could be a case of one of the ways of portraying the Great Mother as the protectress of the city. Placing Cybele among the highest orders of the Olympic gods is in accordance with her character and her status in Rome. Considering the syncretistic nature of the Great Mother, it is also possible that we are following an example of assimilating the two goddesses. In fact, Tyche enriches her character with the aspect of sovereignty over life and death in the Hellenistic period. She grew to be protectress of many cities, certainly most well known as Tyche of Antioch.[221] However, there are not any known examples of syncretism between Cybele and Tyche. Together, they are depicted only on a statue from an unknown location, now in the National museum in Bucurest (fig. 38),[222] where Tyche in smaller dimensions is placed on the right side of the throne, holding a cornucopia in her left hand. They might also be depicted together on an altar terracotta base from Sabrata,[223] the sides of which are decorated with images of Cybele seated on a throne and placed on a *quadriga*. A female figure, possibly Tyche, with cornucopia in her left hand and with her right hand lifted towards Cybele, is on the front.

There is only one known statue from Histria, the one found in the vicinity of *Nesactium* from the first century or the first half of the second (figs. 5, 6).[224] Cybele sits on a beautifully crafted throne and rests her arms on lion protomes. The head and forearms are missing, while the feet are placed on the back of a lion. Girardi Jurkić drew an analogy with the relief from Stobi where Magna Mater rests her hands on the heads of the lions, but in this case, in full figure.[225] However, by observing the general iconography of Cybele, one can assume that the *Nesactium* sculpture has in fact a unique treatment and that it does not have any direct analogies.

The marble statue of Cybele from *Mursa* (fig. 39)[226] is very similar to the previous sculptures; however, it stands out by the quality of craftsmanship. The Goddess is seated on a throne, dressed in a *chiton* and *himation*. The head and arms are missing, while her feet are resting on the back of a lion. It is very possible that this statue furnished a temple. A clay female figurine from *Mursa*[227] has also been related to the Mother Goddess cult and it is assumed that it represents an image of Cybele, even if there are no attributes alluding to this. The goddess sits on a throne and has a face veil that reaches the ground.

Pannonian iconography of the Mother Goddess cult, being a testament of the conjunction of eastern cults expressed on several monument groups, is especially interesting. The amalgamization of symbols on the monuments of these areas clearly illustrates the exchange of spiritual ideas among similar mystery cults.

One of the specific motifs of the funerary monuments from the Pannonian–Noric region is the upper end of stele with a mask placed between two acroterii shaped as lion heads. Tóth included this group in the catalogue of Pannonian Mother Goddess cult monuments.[228] Most frequently the mask is of a bearded deity (Serapis), or of a male head with a Phrygian hat; sometimes the mask is substituted with a *calathos* or with a *cista*, or can even be found combined. Female heads between lions are not rare and are often identified as the head of Cybele. There are several finds of such monuments from Croatia. The fragment of the upper part of a stele from *Mursa* (fig. 40)[229] has a lion on the right side of the woman's head. We see a woman's head with a *calathos* flanked with lions on the upper part of the stele from Popovac (fig. 41).[230] The upper part of the stele from Gabajeva greda (fig. 42)[231] is not finished; therefore it is difficult to recognise the face with *calathos* in the middle. It could represent Cybele or even Medusa. We know of one other stelae with this kind of modelling at the upper end, the one from Gornji Bukovec (fig. 43).[232]

One iconographical characteristic common to these monuments is the ram's head under a lion's paw, a motif that is included in the Mother Goddess iconography.

---

[218] Medini 1981b, n° 68.
[219] Reisch 1913, 119-121, fig. 33; Schober 1923, 215; Medini 1978, 744-5, Pl. 155,1; Vermaseren 1966, 37; Vermaseren 1977a, 143; Medini 1981b, n°24; Vermaseren 1989, n°147.
[220] Lanza 1855, Pl. 2; Abramić 1950, 297-289; Cambi 1965, 57-8, Pl. XVIII-XIX; Medini 1981b, n° 63.
[221] Mitropoulou 1996, 157.
[222] Vermaseren 1977b, n° 37.
[223] Vermaseren 1986, n° 59.
[224] Mlakar 1978, 56; Girardi Jurkić 1999, 3.8.3.

[225] 1972, 52.
[226] Pinterović 1967b, 67-79, tab. 1.; Selem 1980 207f, 15, pl. XXXVII; Vermaseren 1989, n° 124; Tóth 1989, n° 111.
[227] Pinterović 1967b, 72; Selem 1980 209, 17, pl. XXXVIII; Vermaseren 1989, n° 125; Tóth 1989, n° 112.
[228] 1989, *Apendix*, 116-119.
[229] Pinterović 1967b, 73; Selem 1980, 208, 16; Tóth 1989, 118.
[230] Pinterović 1967b, 73; Tóth 1989, n° 26; Kulenović and Muštra 2002, T. I, 4.
[231] Kulenović and Muštra 2002, 143-152, T. I, 1.
[232] Gregl 1996, n° 5.

This specific representation can be found on several funerary monuments in the lapidarium of the Archaeological museum in Zagreb – the ones from Odra (fig. 44),[233] Donji Čehi (fig. 45),[234] *Siscia* (figs. 46, 47)[235] and the tombstone of Lucius Egnatuleus Florentin (fig. 48)[236] whose provenance is not certain, but it is believed that it came from *Siscia* or *Andautonia*. Selem considered this motif as part of the iconography of Serapis[237] despite the fact that the ram is not typical of the cultic imagery of this god, while the lion has a subordinate function. The ram and especially the lion are, on the other hand, frequently seen in the Mother Goddess iconography. In the analysis of this way of combining these two symbols, we will rely on the reflection of Migotti.[238] According to her, the lion overpowers the ram, the metaphor of Attis, in order to ensure his rebirth. An idea of immortality of the soul can be recognised and it is in correspondence with the funeral character of these monuments.

We follow a specific iconographical phenomenon in the Danubian provinces from Roman times. A group of votive object, although incorporated among the monuments of the cult of the Danubian rider,[239] can be considered within the frame of our study regarding the central figure of the Great Goddess flanked with horse riders. The identity of this goddess is not accurate, but her origin is undoubtedly oriental.[240] Perhaps this female figure represents the general concept of the Great Goddess and combines all those known in this region. The Great Goddess is often connected with the rider. The exact correlation is confirmed on the Nesactian sculptures as well (fig. 49).[241] The figure of a horse-rider within the cult iconography of Cybele is seen on the clay plaques from Samothrace, found in the west sanctuary (fig. 50).[242] Here, this figure is connected with Dardanus, the mythological consort of Cybele, with whom she had a son – Koribas.[243]

The Danubian rider expresses the aspect of the warrior, which is agreeable with other figures of warriors found in the mythology and iconography of the Mother Goddess cult. The complexity of the display on Pannonian votive monuments demonstrates the iconography of numerous cults. Besides the cult of Cybele there are those of Jupiter Dolichenus, Isis, the Dioskouroi and the Kabiri.[244] In the wealth of cultic imagery that these objects offer, Mother Goddess symbols can be recognised as well. Therefore this group has to be considered when studying the development of the cult and its influence on local religious traditions. The largest number of monuments from this iconographical group are the plates from Pannonia, while the examples found in the territory of the Republic of Croatia are the most representative ones. There are the ones from Dalj (fig. 51),[245] Vinkovci (fig. 52),[246] Vukovar,[247] from *Mursa*,[248] and three from *Siscia* (fig. 53).[249] There are also two relief marble plates from *Siscia* (figs. 54, 55)[250] with similar representations belonging to this group of monuments, as well as the one from Gračanica (fig. 56).[251] Marble plates of this type are found in Dalmatia – several from *Salona* (figs. 57-63)[252] and one from Čitluk (fig. 64).[253] They are not typical for this region and were probably brought from the Danubian provinces along with the recruited soldiers.[254]

The votive function as well as the iconographic narration reveals the strong mystery character of these cultic objects. We follow allegorical depictions and depictions of the ritual, but also some mystery symbols and deities. The material out of which these objects are made, lead, additionally alludes to their mystic quality and their probable magical use. In order not to go far from the theme of this study, we will point only to the elements borrowed from the Mother Goddess cult system. Above all, there are the depictions with an allusion of *taurobolius* or *criobolius*,[255] the ritual that might have been accepted only after the second century, when it began to exist within the framework of the Mother Goddess system. Another possible element taken from the cult of the Great Mother is the ritual fish meal.[256] The fish is a part of the imagery on the votive stone of Servilia Copiesilla from Salona, who erected an *aedem* dedicated to the Great Mother. As well as the inscribed field, on the right side of this monument there is a fish, a vessel, and a dog; on the left there is a dolphin, a patera and another dog.[257] This symbolic compilation is not

---

[233] Rendić – Miočević 1993, 28-31; Gregl and Migotti 2000, 130-1, fig. 8.
[234] Gregl 1996, n° 1; Gregl and Migotti 2000, Fig. 7.
[235] Katančić 1826, 440; CIL III, 3985; Gregl and Migotti 2000, 119-164.
[236] Brunšmid 1909, 163-164, fig. 358.
[237] Selem 1980, 58.
[238] Gregl and Migotti 2000, 153.
[239] Iskra-Janošić 1966, 49-68.
[240] Tudor 1969, 99-109.
[241] Kovač 1992, 76, fig. 25.
[242] Lawall 2003, 97-99.
[243] Lawall 2003, 99.
[244] Tudor 1976, 179.
[245] VHAD XVI 1935, 64, fig. 4; Wenzel 1961, 91; Iskra-Janošić 1966, 19, tab. II, fig. 1; Tudor 1969, n° 132. Pl. LXIII.
[246] AEMÖ III 1879, 23, n° 2, AEMÖ 127, n° 8; VHAD VI 1902, 149, fig. 76; AE XXIII 1903, 353, 58; Iskra-Janošić 1966, III 2, tab. IV, fig. 1; Tudor 1969, n° 137, Pl. LXV.
[247] AE XXIII 1903, 347, 47; Iskra-Janošić 1966, I, 8; Tudor 1969, n° 141.
[248] AE 1905, 12, n° 73; Tudor 1969, n° 145.
[249] The oval votive plate (AE XXIII 1903, 335, n° 60; VAHD VIII 1905, 124; Iskra – Janošić 1966, IV, 8; Tudor 1969, 162, Pl. LXXIV); The rectangular votive plate is identical with the one from Dalj (AEMÖ III 1879, 171, n° 7; AE XXIII 1903, 348, n° 49; VAHD VIII 1905, 121, fig. 3; Iskra – Janošić 1966, I, 11Tudor 1969, 163); and another rectangular shape (Tudor 1969, 164).
[250] The oval plate (AE XXIII 1903, 336, 33; Tudor 1969, 160, Pl. LXXIII); the fragment of a marble oval votive plate (VHAD XVI 1935, 65, n° 14; Tudor 1969, 161, pl. LXXIII).
[251] Pinterović 1975, 131-133, fig.1.
[252] We know of seven plates, only one of which is in relatively good condition, while the others are fragmentary (Abramić 1940, 299-302, n° 1-7, pl. XIX 1,2, XX 1-5; Tudor 1969, 106-112).
[253] ÖJh XVII 1914, 148, fig. 135; Will 1955, 315, fig. 63; Tudor 1969, 113.
[254] Tudor 1976, 159.
[255] Tudor 1976, 237-244.
[256] Tudor 1976, 208-212.
[257] CIL III, 13903; BASD XVIII 1895, 3; Kubitschek 1896, 87; Drexler in Rocher, *Myth.Lex.* II, col. 2922; Hepding 1903, 189; Dölger 1922, 442; Graillot 1912, 493; Dessau, 1916, 4106; Vermaseren 1977a, 143; Schillinger 1979, 63, 42; Medini 1981b, n° 40; Vermaseren 1989, n° 167; Šašel Kos 1999, 83.

often found in the iconography of the cult, but neither are these symbols singular. This might allude to the mystery aspect of the cult, considering the chthonic symbolism of the dog, and also of the fish, which was commonly eaten during mystery rituals.

Attis

The figure of Attis was accepted in all of the Roman provinces, although not without certain differences in accordance to the religious conceptions and tradition of different peoples, adding to this the influences of other familiar cults. These differences are evidenced in the local iconography. The image of Attis within the cult heritage can be observed as a separate unit, not necessarily connected to the Great Mother. Moreover, in some cases Attis was singled out of the Mother Goddess cult and circulated as a separate idea of chthonic and funeral character. The iconographical diversity of Attis is sufficient in order to serve as a subject of an integral study.

The heterogeneity of the iconography of Attis finds its pattern, above all, in the abundance and variety of the mythological heritage, but also in the allegorical interpretations of the philosophers of later antiquity, where his image went through a great change evolving from a god subject to vicissitudes, to a celestial god, reaching his final apotheosis when elevated to the higher, solar level of his nature. In the iconography, he shows signs of Greek figuration during their colonisation of Asia Minor. He is a handsome Phrygian youth or *Phryx puer* as Ovid (*Met.* 4, 223) and Arnobius (1, 42) have represented him.[258] He is usually dressed in a *tunica manicata* with a belt below his waist and long tight trousers – *anaxyrides*, typical of oriental costume. On his head he has the ubiquitous Phrygian hat with earflaps that often reach his shoulders or are tight below his chin. His feminine beauty was emphasized and his youthful face with curls of hair beneath the hat. Sometimes he was even depicted as an hermaphrodite and with women breasts.[259] His bisexuality is in fact a reflection of his emasculation – the main motif in his myth and cult and an inspiration for Roman philosophy and art.

The primary iconographical type of Attis shepherd is based upon the Phrygian version of the myth,[260] as well as on the Roman version of the myth from Pessinunt known from the Ovid's Fasti (4, 221-244).[261] It seems that the so called Lydian version of the myth of Attis was never an inspiration for the artistic expression of the Mother Goddess cult.[262] Attis was never depicted as hunting or aristocratic. The main attributes that classify Attis as a shepherd are his shepherd's crook or *pedum*, and the *syrinx*. These are, together with the Phrygian hat, his main symbols and can be found on the cult monuments, indicating Attis even without his figural depiction.[263]

Unlike the representations of Cybele that are quite canonical in these regions, the image of Attis offers many variations and a rich symbolical structure. Attis's name is completely absent from Croatian epigraphy, therefore we cannot determine anything about how this god was accepted among the local population. We are left to apprehend his status only through analysis of his representations. The greatest number of finds is certainly from the province of Dalmatia. Attis's character is above all funerary, so his image is generally carved on tombstones or found in graves. He is mostly present on reliefs, but also exists in the round, made in marble and bronze.

The earliest representations of this oriental god are presumably the ones on the tombstones from *Tilurium* from the first half of the first century B.C. and belonging to the soldiers of the VII legion.[264] We recognise him by his typical mourning posture, found very often in Croatia. The military was particularly devoted to the Mother Goddess cult and spread it further throughout the province. In *Burnum*, where the Ninth Legion camped, thecult was an important component of spiritual life, being a part of the official imperial cult.[265] The Mother Goddess gained similar status in *Iader* and *Senia*.[266] Knowing the position of *Salona* as a spiritual centre of the province of Dalmatia, it is understandable that the largest number of representations of Attis, dated in the widest chronological spectrum, comes from this city. The cult came here probably in the time of the intensive colonisation during the reign of Augustus. In the second century *Salona* became the centre of the Mother Goddess religion in the province, with an institution of the *archigallus* and influencing the whole territory of Dalmatia.[267] It is also important to consider the devastation of the monuments during the acceptance of Christianity. So far, we know of four statues of Attis, believed to be products of the Salonitan workshop.[268] The rest of the sculptures from the coastal area are found in *Tragurium*,[269] *Hadra*,[270] and we also know of a sculpture

---

[258] For other epithets of Attis see Hepding 1903, 206-210.
[259] Vermaseren 1987, n° 667.
[260] Pausanias (7.17. 10-12); Arnobius (*Adv. Nat.* 5.5 -7).
[261] See Hepding 1903, 18ff.
[262] This euhemeristic version of the myth was documented by Herodotus (*Hist.* 1. 34-45). See Hepding 1903, 5ff.
[263] Best examples of the non-figural depiction of Attis are on the *taurobolic* altars of late antiquity.
[264] The stele of the unknown rider (Medini, 1981b, n° 75); The stele of Caius Longinus (CIL III 9737; Hofman 1905, 57-58, n° 45, fig. 37; Medini 1981b, n° 76; Tončinić 2004, n° 34); The stele of Cnaeus Domitius (CIL III 2710=9726; Hofman 1905, n° 43; Medini 1981b, n° 77; Tončinić 2004, n° 12).
[265] Medini 1989a, 255-284.
[266] Medini 1981b, 389-90.
[267] CIL III 2920a; Medini 1981a, 15-28.
[268] Along with the three known statues of Attis (Medini 1981b, n° 51-53), there is another recently discovered example (Cambi 2003, 513, fig. 3).
[269] The small stone head (AEMÖ IX 1885, 57; Graillot 1912, 493, n. 1; Medini 1981b, n° 26; Vermaseren 1989, n° 150); and the fragment of a statue of Attis (BASD XXVII 1904, 22, pl. IV; Cambi 1980, n° 10, 11, 956; Medini 1981b, n° 27; Vermaseren 1989, n° 151).
[270] Medini 1977, 195-205; Medini 1978, 747-750, tab. 156, 1-3; Medini 1981b, n° 22; Vermaseren 1989, n° 144.

of *Attis tristis* from *Tarsatica*.²⁷¹ Two bronze statuettes²⁷² and two bronze appliqués from the second or third century with the image of Attis came from *Salona*,²⁷³ while a rather exceptional example of Attis *mutilans* was found in *Andetrium*.²⁷⁴ Attis's image is often seen on Salonitan funerary monuments. The only depictions of Attis from the late third and fourth century are on the sarcophagi from *Salona*.²⁷⁵ A distinct worship of the cult within the province of Dalmatia was attested in *Aenona*. Here, beside six appliqués with the image of Attis, a stone head depicting this god was found.²⁷⁶ Although there are no finds of the Great Mother from this antique city, it is highly possible that her cult was celebrated. We find proofs for this claim from the later, baroque period when here a statue of St. Marie was ritually washed in the sea, an echo of the ritual *lavatio*, part of the festival of the Great Mother.²⁷⁷

The early acceptance of the cult was also attested in Histria, where it came as a result of the influence of Aquileia, the main centre of the Tenth Italic Region of *Venetia et Histria*. The largest concentration of monuments with the image of Attis in Histria is to be found in the *Pola* array. His earliest depiction is on a tombstone of Obellia Maxima from the first century,²⁷⁸ but can also be recognized on two identical funerary cippi from later years of the same century.²⁷⁹ Besides one life-size statue,²⁸⁰ we know of a head of this god from *Pola* (fig. 65).²⁸¹ Another head from Histria, but from an unknown site has been documented (fig. 66)²⁸² and allegedly there was a bronze figurine found in *Nesactium*, now unfortunately lost.²⁸³

The finds from Pannonia tells us that the figure of Attis in this region was adopted later than in Dalmatia and that different spiritual influences affected his local development. While following the traces of the cult towards the interior, we see that the symbolism of the figure of Attis is altered. Besides one mourning Attis from these parts, we know only of bronze statues of the oriental god – one bust from the second²⁸⁴ and three figurines from the third century.²⁸⁵

Characteristics of the iconography, symbolism and allegorical representations of Attis

Attis in the provinces did not have the reputation he enjoyed in Rome or in the larger centres. His local conception is just a rudimentary understanding of the philosophical and spiritual dimensions of his nature. Still, his iconography in provincial art is distinct, with certain symbols and allegorical representations which reveal the mythological-ritual consistency of his divine image. Special attention will be given to this symbolism.

We will begin the analysis of the iconography of Attis with the form most frequent in the region – *Attis tristis*. This iconographical type is regularly found in southeast Dalmatia, where we follow a certain development. According to the differences in the appearance of the attributes, as well as the chronological differences, Medini isolated four types of *Attis tristis* in this province.²⁸⁶ He also raised several questions which we will focus on here – the question of when this type occurred; how was it incorporated in the sepulchral art of the province of Dalmatia; and whether and how it changed its meaning during the Roman Empire.²⁸⁷

Attis tristis, according to Medini, arrived in the territory of Dalmatia with soldiers of eastern origin.²⁸⁸ It is not certain whether Attis was here known in the context of the Mother Goddess cult, or was present independently, transmitting a different religious message. One aspect of Attis's representation relates to monumental tombstones (figs. 67, 68) with motifs of *porta inferi* formed out of four panels. In the lower panels there is an *Attis tristis* depicted antithetically and with no attributes, with the usual posture – crossed legs, head leaned on one hand, while the other hand rests on his stomach for support. In the upper panels there are lion-head door knockers. In the pediment of one of the tombstones from *Tilurium* there is a winged head of a Medusa. It was of apotropaeic function, which, in the case of the motif of *porta inferi*, *Attis tristis* and the lion heads also had. This motif spread further from *Tilurium* to the region between Narona and *Burnum*, exclusively on military funerary monuments. However, the image of the mourning oriental god is now lacking.²⁸⁹ This motif originates from Asia Minor,

---

²⁷¹ Graillot 1912, 491; Medini 1993, 2.
²⁷² A naked Attis leaning against a pillar (Jelić 1894, 169; Medini 1981b, n° 54; Vermaseren 1989, n° 163) and an example with an open tunica (Medini 1981b, n° 55).
²⁷³ Medini 1981b, n° 56, n° 57.
²⁷⁴ Popović, Mano Zisi, Veličković and Jeličić 1963, 100, n° 129; Vermaseren 1977a, 142, fig. 78; Medini 1981b, n° 73; Vermaseren 1989, n° 149; Žanić Protić 1988, 35, T. VI, 35.
²⁷⁵ Medini 1981, n° 60; Cambi 1960, n° 11, n° 12, 60-62.
²⁷⁶ Medini 1989b, 19-31.
²⁷⁷ Belamarić 1998, 65.
²⁷⁸ Carli 1794, 193; Kandler 1855, 262; Reichel 1983, 4, n° 84; Weisshäupl 1901, 202; Gnirs 1915, 270; Sticotti 1914, 213; Degrassi 1970, 625; Vermaseren 1978, n° 248; Girardi Jurkić 1999, 3.9.5.
²⁷⁹ Reichel 1983, n° 93, n° 94; Gnirs 1915, 91, n° 326, n° 327; Swoboda 1969, 204, n° 17; Vermaseren 1978, n° 246; Girardi Jurkić 1999, 3.9.6, 7.
²⁸⁰ Jurkić 1978, T. I; Girardi Jurkić 1999, 3.9.1.
²⁸¹ Swoboda 1969, 203f, n° 13, fig. 4; Vermaseren 1978, n° 245; Girardi Jurkić 1999, 3.9.2.
²⁸² Girardi Jurkić 1999, 3.9.3.
²⁸³ Sticotti 1934, 332; Vermaseren 1978, n° 251; Girardi Jurkić 1999, 3.9.4.

²⁸⁴ Brunšmid 1914, n° 53; Popović, Mano Zisi, Veličković and Jeličić 1963, 99, n° 126; Selem 1980, n° 17, t. XVIII; Vermaseren 1989, n° 121; Cambi 2002, 115.
²⁸⁵ Attis with a mask in his lifted right arm (Brunšmid 1914, n° 54; Selem n° 11, t. XXXVI); Attis with a mask above his head (Brunšmid 1914, n° 55; Selem n° 12, t. XXXVI); Attis with his right arm above his head (Brunšmid 1914, n° 56; Selem n° 13, t. XXXVI).
²⁸⁶ The first type is without attributes and appears the earliest; the second one has the pedum downwards; the third type is Attis with a torch; the fourth one is rare and it is shown as a winged spirit of death (Medini 1981b, 33-43).
²⁸⁷ Medini 1981b, 109.
²⁸⁸ Medini 1981b, 387-388.
²⁸⁹ Medini 1981b, 118.

although there are opposite opinions that the motif was defined in central or northern Italy.[290] The door, on the other hand, is a universal metaphor of secrets and a symbol of passage and the beyond, usually guarded by lions and seen in every culture of the Mediterranean and the East.

The sepulchral character of the cult can be perceived in the early period of its development, on Phrygian rock monuments where the Great Goddess had a protective function as a custodian over graves and protected the earthly residence of the dead from violation.[291] Attis offered the same protection. His name can be found on monuments as a part of the neo-Phrygian protective formula.[292] We follow similarities between Attis and other figures who likewise had a protective role on tombs from Lydia and Antioch,[293] and whose name is also connected with the local epigraphical tradition. Attis, unlike the Great Mother whose jurisdiction is the Earth, guards the souls on their way to the Underworld. The motif of the door leading to the afterlife is especially common in Asia Minor in Roman times. Among the most representative examples from Cotyaeum we see Attis with a goat and a cornucopia, while Heracles stands as his opposite, additionally emphasising the chthonic aspect of this motif.[294]

The iconographical type of *Attis tristis* can also be recognised among the votive terracottas from Macedonian and Cilician necropolises from the second century B.C.,[295] as well as on those from the Palatine from the first century B.C.[296] made after the same pattern. The attributes of *Attis tristis* are, as already mentioned, the pedum and the torch. The pedum indicates Attis as shepherd, the leader of souls towards the Underworld. This allegorical image of the god fits naturally within the context of the symbolic repertoire of the funeral monuments. The torch, on the other hand, is traditionally connected with Mithras and his dadophores and it is considered that in Roman times they additionally influenced the development of *Attis tristis*. However; the torch in the antique iconography is in the hands of women. If we look at the entire Mother Goddess iconography, we can see that the torch as an attribute follows the Great Mother from Hittite times. In the early examples a woman standing besides the Goddess is holding the torch, while in Hellenistic depictions it is in the hands of Hecate. A triad of Hermes and Hecate together with Cybele is a common illustration of initiation rituals. Hermes, now as Mercury, remained a part of this triad in Roman art, but instead of Hecate, we see Attis. This is another possible way that the torch became part of the symbolic structure of Attis. It designates the chthonic aspect of Attis and, above all, his mystic character.

The funerary symbolism of Attis has been gained according to the mystery-ritual content of his cult. Mystic interpretation of Attis in the Roman March festivals consists of the recognition of the ancient element of the divine vicissitude as a paradigm of dying. It can be said that the main determinant of the public rites of Attis is the recollection of his death that leads the initiated into higher states of consciousness. By experiencing death through a series of ceremonies one passes the same way that the deity passed. Instead of the Mother, Attis himself mourns over his death and over the death of the deceased above whose grave he dwells. In time, *Attis tristis* underwent an evolution from a figure of mythological-ritual character to a symbolic figure. In later Roman times, the iconographical type of *Attis tristis* on funerary monuments gained a different value and no longer existed as a symbol of the cult or rituals related to death, but instead expressed the moment of sorrow and mourning over the deceased.[297] He becomes depersonalised and loses the connection with the theology of the Great Mother. The tombstones from *Tilurium*, as well as all the monuments of a sepulchral character on which *Attis tristis* is depicted, belong to a large group of finds from the western Roman provinces. These monuments are particularly frequent in neighbouring Pannonia, but also in Germania, Gaul and Hispania. In the light of new researches, a rather different way of seeing this iconographical type has emerged. In fact, it is plausible that this image does not represent the Phrygian god at all, but was used as a particular funeral motif of the Orientals who travelled to the western provinces and died there.[298] Cambi also doubts that the image of Attis appears on these funeral monuments, emphasising at the same time the complexity of this matter.[299]

As well as in relief, we also find *Attis tristis* in sculpture – e.g the examples from *Pola* (fig. 69), *Salona* (figs. 70, 71) and *Traugurium* (fig. 72). A great number of sculptures of *Attis tristis* are found all over the province of Pannonia, although within the territory of the Republic of Croatia only the example from Siscia is known.[300] Among the Croatian figures of *Attis tristis*, the above-mentioned one on the funerary monument of Obellia Maxima from *Pola* can be included (fig. 73).[301] He is depicted in his typical mourning attitude and placed on the right side of the rectangular aedicule with the image of the deceased. On the left side there is another image, in

---

[290] In the older literature the opinion that the motif originates from Asia Minor prevails (Hofman 1905, 54-57; Patsch 1908, 105; Rendić Miočević 1989, 578; Medini 1984a, 112-114). For the motif originating from central or northern Italy see Righini 1965, 393; Susini 1985, 86-88; Cambi 2002, 150.
[291] Sfameni Gasparro 1985, 90.
[292] The form τετικμένος ATTIC AΔEITOY I which is equivalent to the Greek continental form κατηραμένος Ἄττι ἔστω (Sfameni Gasparro 1985, 90, n. 21) i ΤΙΑΜΑΣ which is equivalent to the form καταχθόνιος (Vermaseren 1987, n° 113) often found in the epigraphy.
[293] Lane III 1976, 51-2.
[294] Vermaseren 1987, n° 140.
[295] Vermaseren 1966, 18.
[296] Vermaseren 1977c, n° 12-199.

[297] Sfameni Gasparro 1985, 93.
[298] Landskron 2005, 121-130.
[299] Cambi 2005b, 54.
[300] Tóth 1989, n° 12.
[301] Carli 1794, 193; Kandler 1855, 262; Reichel 1893, 4, n° 84; Weisshäupl 1901, 202; Gnirs 1912, 270; Sticotti 1914, 213; Degrassi 1970, 625; Vermaseren 1978, n° 248; Girardi Jurkić 1999 II, 3. 9. 5.

which Vermaseren recognised a phallus.[302] Considering the symbolism, the funerary cippi with the figure of Attis *tristis* (fig. 74) reveal even more.[303] The god here is again without any attributes, on the front of an aedicule with columns, an epistyle and a pediment. The monuments are almost identical. On their sides there is a relief decoration of kantharoi, vines with grapes, and birds. The columns from both sides of the aedicule are decorated with a stylized pine tree with a pinecone at the top.

The tree is the main motif in the myth and the cult of Attis, and therefore in his iconography. Not only does he die under the tree, but he was born from the fruit of a tree. Nana conceived Attis at the moment when she placed the almond (Pausanias) or the pomegranate (Arnobius) in her lap. But, in Attis's iconographical repertoire only the pine tree is present. On *arbour intrat*, the seventh day of the public rites in March, the pine tree was brought into the temple, placed on a throne and mourned. It signified the dead god. This ceremony was led by the college of *dendrophoroi*, constituted by the emperor Claudius during the reforms of the cult. On the eve of *pannychis* or *mesonyction*, the pine tree was buried in memory of the burial of Attis in Pessinunt.[304] According to Macrobius (*Sat.*, 1, 21, 10) this is the ritual of *catabasis*, the same held during the Eleusinian mysteries. It is highly likely that the texts of Clement of Alexandria[305] and Firmicus Maternus[306] refer to this night and that one part of the iconographical symbolism of Attis was created after the holy liturgical objects. Attis's image was therefore enriched with the holy instruments through which one could have reached the religious mystery. The young god is often presented leaning against a tree, on which the instruments – syrinx, timpani and cymbals are hanging as reminders of the music and the frenetic dance, the key elements of the rituality of the cult. The pine is an allusion to the basic spiritual concept of Attis. Namely, Attis does not return periodically, he is not reborn and his trials end with death, just as at the end of the March festivals the pine tree is set on fire. Sfameni Gasparro sees in the figure of Attis a deity who is not resurrected, but 'survives in death' and by his example offers consolation, in that his death is necessary for life to continue in a different form.[307]

The pine cone is a well-known funeral symbol, not only in relation to the Mother Goddess religion, but in other oriental cults such as the cults of Sabazius and Dionysius,[308] and especially present in human iconography.[309] It can most often be found on the sepulchral monuments in Gaul. Among the funeral monuments from Croatia, this symbol is recognized on the Liburnian cippi from the first century.[310] There are several terracotta lamps shaped like pine cones from *Siscia* and *Mursa* that are connected to the Mother Goddess cult.[311] A great number of them are found in Pannonia and also one in Aquilea. We already mentioned the importance of Aquilea whose spiritual impetus greatly influenced the development of the cult and its iconography in Histria, but as it seems, in Pannonia as well. The pine cone is a symbol of vegetative regeneration and new life. It is an emblem of immortality and thus often deposited in graves. In the myth, Cybele took the pine cone with her in the cave where she was mourning the death of Attis. In relation to Attis, the pine cone could also represent the *glans penis*, if we only think of the terracotta from the Palatine among which there are both symbols present and similar between themselves (fig. 75, 76). The symbolic composition on the handle of the bronze patera from northern France directly points to the connection of Cybele and Attis with the pine cone (fig. 77).[312]

Bronze cast appliqués from several locations of coastal Dalmatia form a separate group of funeral finds connected with Attis.[313] The face of Attis with Phrygian hat and curly hair is depicted (fig. 78-84). There are altogether 14 of them, out of which 6 are found in *Aenona* and the surrounding area. Among them there are the above-mentioned ones from *Salona*, while the rest came from *Blandona* (fig. 85), *Aequum*, *Diluntium* and *Burnum*. To this group an appliqué with similar craftsmanship from Aquilea can be added, now in the archaeological collection 'Benko Horvat' (fig. 86),[314] as well as the one from *Siscia* (fig. 87), part of the archaeological collection of Mateja Pavletić.[315] These appliqués were parts of the graves with cremated remains, and were of possible apothropeic use, a frequent phenomenon in Mother Goddess cult societies. So far, a local workshop is unknown; it is assumed that there was one in Aquilea, which was an important centre of the cult. Bronze appliqués with the image of Attis were mainly found in the western Roman provinces, although never in such large numbers as in the province of Dalmatia. Among the ones from Germany, Hispania and Gaul there are some examples of fine craftsmanship and high artistic qualities. Closest in style with the Dalmatian ones is one appliqué from an unknown provenance, now in the Louvre (fig. 88)[316] and one more, found in the Roman villa at Russi, Gallia Cispadana (fig. 89).[317]

Among the full figures of Attis, the stone head from *Hadra* is included, a product of a local workshop dated to the middle of the second century. It differs from others in its unusualness. The novelty are the holes between the

---

[302] 1978, n° 248.
[303] Reichel 1893, 93, 94; Gnirs 1915, 91, n° 326, 327; Swoboda 1969, 204, n° 17; Vermaseren 1978, n° 246; Girardi Jurkić 1999 II, 3. 9. 6,7.
[304] Vermaseren 1977a, 115-116.
[305] (*Protrepticos* 2, 15, 3).
[306] (*De errore profanorum religionum*, 18, 1).
[307] Sfameni Gasparro 1985, 125.
[308] Sfameni Gasparro 1985, 100.
[309] Lane III 1976, 104-5.

[310] Suić 1952, 59; Cambi 2002, 156; Fadić 2003, 97-131.
[311] Tóth 1989, 17, 18, 113.
[312] Vermaseren 1986, n° 467.
[313] Medini 1986, 109-125.
[314] Koščević 2000, 119, n° 197.
[315] Balen, Demo, Ožanić, Radman – Livaja, Rendić – Miočević, Uranić 2003, 88, n° 161.
[316] Vermaseren 1989, n° 118.
[317] Susini 1978, 25.

forehead and the Phrygian hat, which does not have the usual curved top but is of pointed appearance (fig. 90).[318] It has been assumed that flowers were put in the holes to decorate the statue during the celebrations of Attis's festivals, or to be more precise, during *hilaria*. Medini compared this find with the well-known statue of reclining Attis from Ostia with a garland of flowers on his head.[319] However, we believe that there is a closer analogy, also from Ostia. In the vicinity of the temple of Cybele a marble head with seven holes on the border of the hat was found (fig. 91). Vermaseren agreed with Cumont that it is in fact a head of Mithras.[320] In the iconography of Attis there are no similar examples known to us, therefore there is a great possibility that the head from *Hadra* is also a representation of the god Mithras.

On the basis of the similarities with the local god Sylvan, Garašanin and Zotović believed that Attis was assimilated with this shepherd deity, especially in the eastern parts of the province of Dalmatia.[321] This epychoric god was especially worshipped among the Delmats, who lived mainly from cattle breeding.[322] The naturalistic character of Sylvan suits the vegetative character of Attis. On the relief slab from Pridraga from the third century (fig. 92) Cambi saw an example of a syncretization of Sylvan with Attis.[323] His main argument was the Phrygian hat on the head of this figure. This interpretation was not acceptable to Vermaseren based on several objections.[324] However, we may not be too far wrong if we assume that in the hearts and minds of the population within these areas there was an assimilation of these two gods. Perhaps Selem's consideration that music is the only link between Sylvan and Attis, and that there was no actual syncretism but a sole encounter,[325] is the most accurate one.

Attis from the Croatian material is known to be depicted together with Cybele only on the relief from the *Burnum* Forum. On the frieze from the aedicule that belonged to the sanctuary, the Phrygian god is shown under a tree, at the moment when Cybele finds him after his emasculation (fig. 93). From the left and also from the right side of the composition, the frieze is framed with two figures of *Attis tristis*.[326] On the northeast side of the Forum, on the frieze that stood as a converse to this aedicule, Reisch recognised Adonis and placed him in relation with the above-mentioned composition.[327] Attis and Adonis certainly share common elements in their mythological and spiritual structure. Furthermore, the myth of Adonis was most probably created under the influence of the myth of Attis. They both belong to the same category of vegetative deities that underwent a certain period of suffering and were commemorated with nocturnal rituals and mystery rites where their destinies were mourned.[328] These two gods stand as symbols of cyclical changes of nature, but not without a certain distinction – Attis is a metaphor of a flower picked before it fruits, while Adonis symbolizes ripe fruit, as in fact Eusebius (*Praep. evang.* 3, 11, 12) has compared them.

The bronze figurines of Attis from *Siscia* from the third century have a distinctive iconographical solution (figs. 94, 95). They are representations of Attis as a child with an open *tunica manicata*, holding a mask of the Great Goddess. One of them is holding the mask with his uplifted right hand,[329] while the other has both hands lifted above his head.[330] There are several analogous examples. Vermaseren believes that the bronze statuette found in Marseille is in fact an Etruscan import.[331] The provenance of the others with identical posture is unknown, while they are kept in eminent European museums (figs. 96, 97).[332] We notice that these bronze figures of Attis offer another significant attribute. Selem stressed the significance of the mask through which a theatrical dimension of the cult of Cybele and Attis is transmitted, in this case recognizable in the local iconography.[333] The mask is usually a symbol of Dionysus, the god of theatre, transcended from magical to theatrical use.[334] It was used in the rituals honouring Attis, by means of which the lamentation and the worshipping of the god during *tristia* and *hilaria* were expressed more effectively. On the day of *arbor intrat*, the mask was installed on the pine tree; thereby the tree became Attis himself. Attis is depicted also with the mask of Sabazius, whether dancing on top of it, or leaning upon it, but also with the mask of Sangarius, the personification of the holy river of Pessinunt. The mask as a part of the Mother Goddess iconography is again seen on the find from *Mursa*, placed between two lions.[335] This motif is found in other Pannonian centres of the cult, e.g. *Sirmium*.[336]

The third bronze Attis from *Siscia* is shown dancing, nude again, but this time without a mask, with his right hand above his head (fig. 98).[337] This is a solitary example of *Attis hilaris* from the territory of Republic of Croatia. The dance is, as we know, one of the main

---

[318] Medini 1977, 195-205; Medini 1978, 747-750, tab. 156, 1-3; Medini 1981b, n° 22; Vermaseren 1989, n° 144.
[319] Medini 1977, 197-198.
[320] Vermaseren 1977c, n° 396.
[321] Garašanin 1951, 158; Zotović 1973, 34.
[322] Rendić-Miočević 1989, 462.
[323] 1968, 131-141.
[324] Vermaseren's doubt is based on two attributes – the snake that this god holds in his left hand that is not typical for the iconography of Attis and the *penis erectus* which is not in accordance with the divine nature of Attis (1989, n° 143).
[325] 2005, 426-427.
[326] Medini 1989a.
[327] 1913, 119-121.

[328] Burkert 1987, 75.
[329] Brunšmid 1914, n° 54; Selem 1980, n° 11, t. XXXVI; Selem 1981, 187-194, fig. 2; Vermaseren 1989, n° 118; Tóth 1989, n° 13.
[330] Brunšmid 1914, n° 55; Selem 1980, n° 12, t. XXXVI; Selem 1981, 187-194, fig. 3; Vermaseren 1989, n° 119; Tóth 1989, n° 14.
[331] Vermaseren 1986, n° 318.
[332] One from Asia Minor, now in the Louvre (Vermaseren 1977b, n° 114), other also in Paris, kept in the collection of the Bibliothèque Nationale (Vermaseren 1977b, n° 113), while the third one is in Berlin, in the Staatliche Museen (Vermaseren 1977b, n° 18).
[333] Selem 1981, 189-198.
[334] Dodds 1956, 94, n. 82.
[335] Tóth 1989, 118, n° 27.
[336] Tóth 1989, n° 32-37.
[337] Brunšmid 1914, n° 56; Selem 1980, n° 13, t. XXXVI; Selem 1981, 187-194, fig. 3; Vermaseren 1989, n° 120; Tóth 1989, n° 15.

elements of the rituals in honour of Attis. He learned it from his guardian, the Great Mother (Julian, *Or.*, 8 (5), 6). His dance is also a reminder of the madness in which Attis castrated himself; inflicted on him by Cybele in fury after his encounter with the nymph. The *galloi* from Pessinunt, following the god's example, danced in frenzy and castrated themselves. The same ritual was performed during the Roman March festivals, on the day called *Sanguem*.[338] *Attis hilaris* stands as a contrast or alternative to *Attis tristis* and completes the idea of his assured survival after death. Attis is dual and bipolar; he is carries with him a certain paradigm of duality and infinite transfiguration of death into life, expressed also in his iconography. His absence and presence in ritual were evoked by lamentation and joy.[339]

We also have some fine examples of bronze figurines with the image of Attis from Dalmatia, two of which were discovered in *Salona* (figs. 99, 100) and dated to the period between the second and the third century. The bronze statuette from *Andetrium* shows Attis kneeling on his right knee and in the act of castration. It is because of this posture that this item is unique within the entire iconography of Attis. The god is in ecstasy, holding a knife in his lifted right hand. The expression on his face makes this statuette exceptionally expressive (fig. 101).

The most exceptional bronze find of Attis from the entire territory of the Republic of Croatia is the one from *Siscia*, now in the Archaeological museum in Zagreb. It is a bronze bust of the young god from the second century with a six-pointed star on the Phrygian hat. Despite the meaning that this bust portrays Mithras,[340] Vermaseren, nevertheless recognised the image of Attis (fig. 102).[341] Medini saw the six-pointed star on the bronze appliqués from Dalmatia as well, although it is questionable whether it is a star or an incrustation of a different kind. We find evidence about the symbolism of the star hat of Attis among the Neo-Platonists. According to Sallustius (1, 4) Cybele saw Attis by the river, fell in love with him and adorned him with a starry hat so he can eternally remain by her side and become the creator of all things that are being born and destroyed. This attribute can also be seen on some of the monuments of mortals.[342] In any event, the six-pointed star is added to the Mother Goddess cult through the Iranian solar and astral theology that propagates the eschatological principle of light.[343] As well as on the hat and clothes of Attis, the six-pointed star can also be seen on the tympanum in the hands of Cybele. This symbol is often seen on the representations of the mystery-initiatory rituals.

Recently, a small bust of the *Blätterkelch* type was discovered in *Siscia*. The figure of the god is placed on a garland of flower petals and has a corona of ivy leaves on its head (fig. 103).[344] Although it suggests more of the Dionysian imagery, the attributes are not unusual for Attis as well. The affirmed importance of the Mother Goddess religion in *Siscia* leads us towards the assumption that this figurine could represent the Phrygian god. We do not have any proof about the presence of the Dionysian cult in this region. The ivy corona is seen on the head of Attis on two earlier terracotta figurines from Cilician Tarsus from the first century (figs. 104, 105),[345] on the marble antefix from Nemausus in Gaul (fig. 106),[346] and on the base of the bronze bust of Attis from Laconian Malea, now in the Louvre.[347] There are six leaves on the ivy corona and they are arranged three on each side of the hat. It is difficult, at the same time, not to think of the six-pointed star on the hat of the god from the previous examples and also the possibility that the ivy leaves are somehow a continuation of the eschatological and solar idea of the oriental god in the province of Pannonia. Ivy is a common element in the Thracian art and present not only in the Dionysian, but also in the Kabiric iconography. It was used during the mystery rituals of these gods, while its use is also known in the Eleusinian mysteries.[348]

We will now return to the Dalmatian funerary monuments in order to examine closely the religious idea that was, together with Attis, present in the local awareness of the worshippers. Among the Salonitan funeral monuments with the image of *Attis tristis* we come across an inscription from the second century, mentioned earlier in the previous chapter and through which we perceived the notion of the immortality of the soul present in the religion and connected with Attis. The inscription is part of the tombstone of a deceased fourteen-year-old boy, Aeronius Firmin. On both sides there is an image of *Attis tristis*, while in the corners there are kantharoi with vines (fig. 107).[349] There is another tombstone with similar decoration from *Salona*, from the same time period, found together with the previous one. Below the framed and inscribed field there are stylized palm leaves, rosettes and a large flower. On the sides of this monument we see two images of *Attis tristis* leaning on the pedum, turned downwards, while the vertical edges are decorated with vines, grapes, leaves and two kantharoi in the lower corners (figs. 108, 109). It is noticeable that the decorative motifs on these monuments have been taken from Dionysian iconography. Here Cambi did not recognize Attis, but an oriental shepherd, the predecessor of the shepherd themes on the later, Christian Salonitan sarcophagi.[350]

---

[338] According to the calendar of Furius Dionysius Filocalus from the year 354, this day was commemorated on the 24th of March (CIL I², 260).
[339] Sfameni Gasparro 1985, 94.
[340] Popović, Mano Zisi, Veličković and Jeličić 1963, 99, n° 126; Cambi 2002, 115.
[341] 1989, 121.
[342] Lane III 1976, 92.
[343] Burkert 2004, 99-124.

[344] I kindly thank my colleague Josip Burmaz for drawing this find to my attention.
[345] Vermaseren 1987, n° 816, n° 836.
[346] Vermaseren 1986, n° 328.
[347] Vermaseren 1982, n° 506.
[348] Маразов 1992, 128, 142.
[349] CIL III, 6384, Hepding 1903, 86, 25; Graillot 1912, 493; Lagrange 1919; 475; Medini 1981b, n° 58.
[350] Cambi 2005b, 103-105.

The decoration of the three-part funeral monument from the beginning of the second century from Sinj, with a possible origin from Gardun,[351] is particularly interesting. The head of Attis with a Phrygian hat in high relief is on the pediment, while the acroterii are shaped as lions, of which only the paws remain. The motifs of a krater and two dolphins are interchanging in the decorative frieze with two masks between the dolphins' tails (fig. 110). The fish is part of the decoration on the altar vowed by Servilia Copiesilla from *Salona*,[352] and on another Dalmatian funeral monument, the one from Lepuri dated to the period between the second and the third century.[353] Besides the figure of *Attis tristis* on the front, there are two fish and five loaves of bread on the back, most likely a depiction of the ritual meal or the liturgy of this cult.

Dolphins and fish are rarely to be seen in the Mother Goddess iconography. They are usually found in the representations of the arrival of the Great Mother in Rome on the terracotta reliefs from the third century,[354] indicating the sea journey of the Phrygian Goddess. On the other hand, fish have an entirely different meaning, which leads to a consideration of the content of the ritual meal in the cult. A winged Attis-Eros on the Hellenistic terracotta statuette from Faiyŭm holds a plate with fish in his lifted right arm,[355] while on the bronze figurine from *Singidunum* from the second or third century, Attis holds a fish by its tail in his right hand and a knife with his left.[356] The image of a funerary Attis on a relief from Romanian Potassia is, besides the syrinx, augmented with a depiction of a fish.[357] This tombstone is dated to the same period as the one from Sinj, which opens the possibility that the fish as an attribute in the iconography of the Mother Goddess cult found in Croatia came via an eastern, continental influence. The fish was, in fact, more sacred to populations living in Mediterranean interiors than it was to those living by the sea.[358] The fish is very important in mystery cults, especially in the cult of the Kabiri.[359] Sacrifice of the fish played an important role in the cult of the Thracian rider, closely connected to the Great Gods of Samothrace.[360] The fish is a key motif in the Christian symbolism, and, as well as being representation of the image of Christ, is also a Eucharistic-soteriological symbol. While observing the funerary symbolism of Attis, it is impossible not to mention early Christian iconography. It is an easy step to see the pagan within Christian iconography.[361] The motif of the fish with five loaves of bread is registered on several early Christian monuments from Croatia – on the lamps from Solin,[362] on the sarcophagus from Trogir, on the relief from Brnaz near Sinj,[363] and on the sarcophagus from Vinkovci.[364]

Finally, we can turn our attention to the Salonitan late antique sarcophagi among which we find the latest depictions of the figure of Attis from the repertoire of the Croatian monuments. On one of them, on the front side and left from the *tabula ansata*, the Phrygian god is in a composition with three goats (fig. 111).[365] Attis is, as with every other deity, identified with his sacrificial animal.[366] In his case it is a goat, from which he eventually got his name. Wild goats in Phrygia were called *attagoi*.[367] A male goat was ritually slaughtered in honour of Attis. According to the Phrygian legend Attis was nursed by a goat, yet this motif was not found in the cult art.[368] On a terracotta figurine from Myrina, Attis rides a goat (fig. 112).[369] His goat-like character was additionally emphasized with the figure of Pan that followed Attis in his sanctuary in Ostia.[370] There is a fine example connecting these two deities on an *oscilum* from the theatre in Orange.[371] Here, on the front, Attis is shown together with Sylenus, while on the reverse we see Cybele with Pan.

On the rest of the sarcophagi one can follow the allegorical representation of Attis Winter within the composition of the Four Seasons – a late iconographical specificity of the image of Attis.[372] Two of these monuments belong to the third century, the time when this particular iconographical conception reached its greatest popularity. The Erotes on the first sarcophagus are on both sides of the *tabula ansata* (fig. 113),[373] while on the other they are depicted on the acroterium of its lid (fig. 114).[374] On the first example, winged Attis Winter is in a group with the Erote of Spring and placed on a high pedestal. In his right hand he is holding an animal by its back legs and a bough in his left. Attis on the acroterium is again winged and holds a bough, but this time with his right hand, while he is leaning against a basket of fruit with his left. In contrast to the first example, here Attis is in a group with the Erote personifying fall. It has to be

---

[351] Medini 1981b, n° 74; Medini 1984a, fig. 3.
[352] CIL III 13903; BASD XVIII 1895, 3; Kubitschek 1896, 87f, n° 4; Graillot 1912, 493; Vermaseren 1977a, 143; Medini 1981b, n° 40; Vermaseren 1989, n° 167.
[353] Medini 1981b, n° 21.
[354] Vermaseren 1977c, n° 340, n° 432.
[355] Vermaseren 1986, n° 20.
[356] Vermaseren 1989, n° 378.
[357] Vermaseren 1974.
[358] Burkert 1983, 207.
[359] Маразов 1992, 147.
[360] Burkert 1983, 210.
[361] Attis, from the iconographical perspective, is in many ways similar to Jesus. They are both shepherds, while the pine tree can be seen as an equivalent of the cross on which Jesus was crucified. There are similarities in the spiritual conception as well. From the eschatological perspective, Attis is also a saviour god. See Fear 1996, 37-50.
[362] De Waal 1894, 3.
[363] Cambi 1977, 94.
[364] Cambi 2002, 273.
[365] Cambi 1970, 60-61, fig. 10-11; Medini 1981b, n° 60; Cambi 2003, 520, fig. 14.
[366] Burkert 1983, 76.
[367] Turcan 1996, In the etymology of Attis's name another interesting fact can be found – the word *atta* which belongs to a group of the so-called 'Lal-wörter' that repeat the consonant, for example mama, papa etc, signifying the paternal aspect. About the 'Lal-wörter' see Fauth 1967, 129-148; about the word *atta* see Chantraine 1986, *s.v.*
[368] Vermaseren 1966, 7-8.
[369] Vermaseren 1987, n° 498.
[370] Vermaseren 1977c, n° 365.
[371] Vermaseren 1986, n° 351.
[372] Vermaseren 1966, 39.
[373] Lanza 1856, 31, T. VIII, 2; Iveković 1910, T. 245; Gorenc 1952, T. 56, 57; Cambi 1960, n° 11; Cambi 2002, 166, fig. 254.
[374] Abramić 1929, 63; Cambi 1960, n° 12; Cambi 2002, 166-7, fig. 255, 256.

noticed that both sarcophagi are imported. The workshop in *Salona* was not familiar with the practice of depicting Attis Winter. The only example of the personification of winter that is the product of a local craftsmanship is, as far as we know, an image of a female hora.[375]

Connecting the four seasons and the zodiac with the iconography of Cybele and Attis is not an unusual feature, but it is not common. *Salona* was indeed well acquainted with the currant fashion that came out of Rome. Cybele, the Goddess of fertility and the changes of the vegetation cycle, was also considered to be a Goddess of the seasons as well. On a Hellenistic altar from Galatia, from the place today known as Seïfi Ören, there is an inscription below the bucranium where an epithet of the Mother is written: Μητρὶ Τετραπροσώπω.[376] The earliest representation of Attis together with the Four Seasons is on the reliefs of the sepulchral monument belonging to the family *Concordia* from Gaul, from the first half of the first century A.D. Here, the image of *Attis tristis* does not personify winter but instead flanks the four spirits of the seasons.[377] Not until later times was Attis incorporated in this composition. The ideological predecessor of Attis Winter was *Attis tristis*, the protector and guardian of graves. His figure was enriched with wings as a reflection of the syncretism with Eros. The most representative achievement of personified winter in the image of Attis is certainly on the 'Dumbarton Oaks sarcophagus' from Rome from the first half of the fourth century (fig. 115).[378] With his right hand, now broken off, he was supposedly holding a basket, a duck or a rabbit, usual symbols of winter in his representations. The left hand is also broken off, but originally was lowered down and with it the god was holding a pedum or a bough. The whole ensemble was made in a style called 'Constantinian classicism'. We find Attis as personified winter on a sarcophagus from Hispanian Emporium, also from the fourth century (fig. 116).[379] The four seasons are also present on the silver lanx from Parabiago.[380] This splendid object offers an especially rich astral symbolism. The astral connotation and the cosmic sense of the figure of Attis have their roots in the concept of the divine transformation of this god.[381] The mythological moment of the disappearance of Attis found an adequate figural expression as personified winter. Attis within the frames of the composition of the four seasons is also depicted as personification of spring on the sarcophagus from the church St. Cecilia in Rome. Unfortunately, it is not preserved – only a drawing of it has survived.[382] If Attis depicted as 'winter' signifies his own death, than it is only logical that as 'spring' he designates the rebirth of life. One can conclude that these allegorical depictions of Attis are analogous to the rituals of *tristia* and *hilaria* in the cycle of the March festivals.

There is one more attribute noticeable in association with the image of Attis winter and connected to the mystery rites – the bough. The bough is a common symbol not only for Eleusinian, but also Dionysian mysteries. Cumont saw in the bough held by Attis winter an emblem of immortality in the context of his eschatological concept.[383] In the repertoire of the Mother Goddess religion the bough is appearing in the hands of Cybele and the *galloi*. He had fallen into death so he can, as Attis, be reborn in a new life.[384]

---

[375] Cambi 1960, n° 17.
[376] Vermaseren 1987, n° 48.
[377] Vermaseren 1986, n° 210.
[378] Vermaseren 1977c, n° 315.
[379] Vermaseren 1986, n° 210.
[380] Musso 1983.
[381] Sfameni Gasparro 1985, 98-99.
[382] Vermaseren 1966, 39, n° 3.
[383] 1942, 388-391.
[384] Sfameni Gasparro 1985, 100.

THE FRESCO FROM ZADAR AND THE MOTIF OF THE CORYBANTES

The fresco from Zadar

Rich in symbols and figures and framed with flower motifs, on the wall of the previously mentioned chamber, southeast from the *Iader* Capitolium, was a fresco painted by a local painter[385] and valued as one of the most important artifacts from antique times within the territory of the Republic of Croatia. The frequent use of yellow, red, green, and especially black, is the argument on which Suić and Medini grounded their opinion that it dates no later than the first decade of the second century and that it is analogous to the third period of the Pompeian style.[386] The Goddess is painted *en face* (fig. 117) on the end of the left side of the wall and is considerably bigger than the rest of the figures. She was recognized by the lions by her side and by the different art and style treatment. The expression on the Goddess' face is stressed by deep shadows, while her hair is braided in *crobylos*. Other figures (figs. 118-123) form a complex compositional structure which indicates the plausibility that a certain ritual was presented. There are at least fourteen figures among which a person who steps with his right foot on a serpent, a bearded old man, a head of a young man with lifted left arm, a young man with a patera in his left hand and a spring of water below him, as well as a *synplegma* of a man and a woman, can be recognized. Placed between a bull and a ram there is a depiction of a Corybant in an ecstatic dance with greaves on his legs, a helmet on his head and a shield in his hand (fig. 124). Tracing this figure not only through iconography but the mythological entirety related to the Great Goddess, one of the numerous aspects of this cult can be comprehended.

The motif of the Corybantes in the iconography of the Mother Goddess cult

The motif of the armed companion of Cybele points to a particular character of this cult, but also to a certain mystery ritual, representing in that way an inevitable part of the entire structure of the Mother Goddess religion. Warriors in the mythological complexity concerning Cybele are usually associated with the Corybantes, prototypes of warriors in the Phrygian-Cretan myth and cult, inventors of the Mother Goddess's holy instrument – the tympanum.[387] According to Diodorus Siculus (5. 48. 2), the Corybantes took their name from Corybas, the son of Cybele and Yasión. This is how he called the group of men that celebrated the Great Mother with orgiastic and secret rites in Phrygia. Ovid (*Fast.* 4. 207-14), on the other hand, wrote that the worshippers using tympana and the cymbals imitated the sound of the Curetes and the Corybantes by banging their arms. The emperor Julian the Apostate (*Orat.* 5.168b), exceptionally fond of the cult, in his Neo-Platonic interpretations described the Corybantes as the lance bearers (δορυφόροι) of Attis. The figure of a warrior is in fact a symbolic transformation of Neolithic hunters into ritual organizations that gravitated around the Great Mother.[388] From the time of its formation until the late-Roman period the opulent iconography of the Mother Goddess religion offers numerous examples where the motif of the armed companion can be found. The attributes of the Corybantes are shield, dagger and helmet, while Euripides in *The Bacchae* (123) gives them the epithet τρικόρυθες, an illusion to their triple plume.[389] Most often the warrior comes in a group of three identical figures (κουρητικὴ τρίας), placed within a rich figural and compositional scheme, but also in simple iconographical solutions, flanking the Goddess.

Depicting Cybele between two acolytes is one of the basic and most widely spread iconographical styles, with long continuity and traceable back to the terracotta figurines from Çatal Hüyük. In much later times, on a sculpture from Boğazköy dated from the late seventh or early sixth century B.C. (fig. 125), Kubaba, with a high polos on her head, is depicted standing between two musicians, with a clear allusion to the use of music during her worship.[390] Cybele, in a similar triad, this time with the Corybantes, which again alludes to music and ecstatic dance, is shown on a terracotta figurine from Egina (fig. 126). The Goddess is seated on a throne with a crown representing a walled city on her head, holding a patera in her right hand and a tympanum in her left.[391] In some cases Attis joins the group. On two roman terracotta lamps from south Italy (figs. 127, 128) busts of Cybele and Attis are shown surrounded by Corybantes. The Goddess is again depicted with her 'city-wall' crown and a tympanum, while Attis holds a syrinx. The Corybantes with helmets and shields, considerably smaller in dimension, are placed above the heads of the deities.[392] We follow a different concept on a terracotta lamp from Britain found in Mitcham, on which Attis is depicted alone, seated on a throne and placed on a carriage, pulled by four goats. Behind one of the goats is a Corybant, dancing and banging his dagger on the shield, with a plumed helmet on his head.[393] The iconographical figure of Cybele, the empress and protectress of cities, is common for all the examples where the armed companion can be seen. In this context, Corybantes can be viewed more in the light of an 'aristocracy' than regular warriors, bearing in mind that arms are, above all, symbolic of higher social classes. One of the basic characteristics of Cybele is her connection with the

---

[385] Cambi 2002, 191.
[386] The fresco is lost from the Archaeological museum in Zadar, therefore we are relying on the existing descriptions made by Suić 1965b, 101-104; Suić 1981, 288; Medini 1981b, n° 15.
[387] Robertson 1996, 269.

[388] Burkert 1979, 120-1.
[389] Robertson 1996, 293.
[390] Naumann 1983, 71-84, Taf. 7, 1.
[391] Vermaseren 1982, n° 527.
[392] Vermaseren 1978, n° 138, n° 144.
[393] Vermaseren 1986, n° 486.

aristocracy and the ruling class. In addition, other divinities with imperial status also follow Cybele and the Corybantes.

The earliest depictions of Cybele together with the armed warriors in more complex compositions date from the fourth century B.C. In the first half of this century, a relief was made in Piraeus with obvious mystery connotations.[394] The whole composition is placed in a naiskos, a Greek contribution in the Goddess's iconography (fig. 129).[395] Cybele is within the temple and on a throne, adored by a bearded man with raised right hand. Behind this scene there are five figures hidden behind a curtain; two women and three armed warriors with helmets and shields, interpreted as nymphs and Curetes. The composition on the relief from Amphipolis, from the same period, is again of standard solution; in Greek style, with naiskos as an architectural frame, the iconographical trend of the times. In front of the right column there is a youth holding a snake and in front of the left a woman with two long torches in both hands – most probably Hermes and Hecata. Placed above each of the figures there is Pan playing a syrinx. Cybele is depicted *en face* on the throne within the temple, with the regular tympanum, patera and lions beside her legs, while the armed Curetes are above her, in the gable of the naiskos.[396] A later funeral slab from the Etruscan city of Luna from the second century B.C. has similar Greek iconographical arrangement, placed in a naiskos (fig. 130). Cybele is again found on a throne, but on the right side of the composition. In front of her are the deceased, a man and a woman. The three Corybantes are behind the curtain, as they are on the relief from Piraeus.[397]

Following the iconographical analogies, we are led towards the Thracian cultural heritage. A relief dedicated to the Thracian Great Mother Goddess, Bendis (fig. 131), shows the same iconographical scheme as the previously described reliefs of Cybele. Bendis stands together with a bearded god, here named as *Dioptes*, while besides them there are two worshippers with smaller dimensions. The scene is set up in the front plane by a curtain, behind which Hermes stands, holding a cornucopia and leading a group of three female figures. In the Thracian mythology Bendis is seen as a royal divinity, directly connected with initiations among the aristocratic circles.[398]

On the famous Hellenistic relief from Lebadeia (fig. 132)[399] one can vividly see the initiatory character of the depicted ritual.[400] In front of the seated Goddess there is a person with a veil, clearly an initiate who is led into her mysteries by Persephone and Dionysus. Behind them follow the usual gathering of mystery gods with their attributes: Pan with a pedum and a syrinx, Hecate with torches, a bearded god with *cornucopiae* and snakes besides his legs. The three Corybantes are placed behind the ritual table, as if they were placed behind a type of curtain. Next in line are the Dioskouroi, and in front of them there are four worshippers in reduced proportions – three women and a man. The procession is going towards the crowned Cybele seated on a throne with her ever-present companion, the lion. The presence of Pan and Dionysus, as well as Demeter and Persephone, reveals that the mysteries of Cybele were close to the Dionysian and Eleusinian ones. It is known that in Lebadeia, besides the Cybele cult, there were mysteries of chthonic and orgiastic character constituted around the figure of Trophonius and the local sanctuary.[401] Plutarch in his *De facie in orbe Lunae* (30, 944ce) places Trophonius together in the same group with Dactyls and Corybantes and sees them as moon spirits, helpers of Kronos and intermediates between men and gods. During the Hellenistic period of emphasised religious syncretism we follow wider symbolism in correspondence with more open communications through which spiritual doctrines were transmitted. The Mother Goddess cult was connected with the Iranian solar and astral theology, therefore Sol was added to the iconography, as well as the motif of the six-pointed star. The eschatological principal of light is now recognisable in the cult of Cybele. Experiencing the light was an important element in the mystery cults, during which one reached the limits of death and divine truth.[402] A golden diadem with engraved figures and their attributes comes from the Palestinian Neapolis (fig. 133).[403] Cybele in a triad with Hermes and Hecate is in the central position. She has *corona muralis* on her head and is flanked with lions. The six-pointed star is on the tympanum which Cybele holds in her hand. Zeus-Jupiter and Helios-Sol are to the right, while to the left are Hera-Juno, Apollo, a female figure, and one of the Curetes.

Another representative relief, this one from the time of Antoninus, offers a rich compositional structure. On the upper part of this monument from the island of Tasos (fig. 134)[404] a procession of gods is depicted with a triad in the middle consisting of Cybele in the centre, Hermes and Hecate with torches. On the left, as well as Hermes, there are Apollo, Leto and Artemis in a row, while on the right, next to Hecate are two pairs – Demeter and Persephone and Aphrodite and Ares. It is possible that Ares is part of the group of the Corybantes or the Dioskouroi. The Roman plaque in stucco from Egypt (fig. 135),[405] obviously made to follow the model of the Greek reliefs from the fourth century B.C., has a similar depiction, but compositionally much richer. In particular, the base of the monument is embellished with the twelve Olympian gods, while the architectural frame is fully decorated with palmetas, lion figures and bulls' heads. Sol is at the top, flanked by three armed Curetes on each

---

[394] Vermaseren 1982, n° 270.
[395] For more about the development of the naiskos in the iconography of Cybele see Rein 1996, 223-237.
[396] Vermaseren 1989, n° 291.
[397] Vermaseren 1978, n° 204.
[398] Маразов 1994, 57-68.
[399] Vermaseren 1982, n° 432; Naumann 1983, 191.
[400] Sfameni Gasparro 1985, 22-3.

[401] See Bonnechere 2003, 169-192.
[402] Burkert 1987, 89-100.
[403] Vermaseren 1987, n° 896.
[404] Vermaseren 1982, n° 528.
[405] Vermaseren 1986, n° 28.

side. Crowned Cybele is on the throne, frontally, Hermes with a caduceus on the right, and Artemis-Hecate with long torches on the left.

The dance of the Corybantes is depicted on one of the most beautiful objects of Roman art made in honour of Magna Mater – the fourth-century silver lanx from Parabiago (fig. 136).[406] It is a real amalgam of different motifs which build a complex allegorical structure. The whole nature and cycle of life are celebrated. Cybele is in the centre of the composition, driving by four magnificent lions on a quadriga, and accompanied by her pareder Attis. The three Corybantes are dancing around Cybele and Attis, banging their swords on their shields. They form a closed circle onto which the other figures are added. Interwoven with the numerous figures that personify day and night, the Seasons, Earth and Water, there is a vast richness of symbols, including the tree of life, a snake wrapped around an obelisk, and the six-pointed star. A hexagonal marble plate from Gaul (fig. 137)[407] kept in the National Library in Paris, once again shows an example of the Corybantic dance. This time a Menada with cymbals joins in. Attis is also present, lying under a tree, and one of the Corybantes is trying to involve the young god in the dance. Cybele is on a throne and reclining on a tympanum decorated with a six-pointed star.

The iconographical background of the presentation of Cybele together with the armed warriors, explained through the symbolic language of the mysteries offers the possibility of interpreting her secret ceremonies, taking into account that the usual accompanying figures, as well as the symbols and the attributes, have clear 'mystery' allusions. The iconographical form of Cybele the Queen and protectress of cities is typical in all the examples where the armed companion is shown. The Corybantes in this context can be looked at as a representation of aristocracy rather than regular warriors, bearing in mind that weapons as a rule are symbols of higher social classes. The other figures have certain characteristics which helps define the exact nature of the mystery ritual in question. Hermes and a woman with torches, or Hecate, are often companions of Cybele in the compositions, together with the Corybantes. With the Goddess they form a triad to which other figures can be added, and imply rituals of a mystery-chthonic nature. At the same time they signify the Hellenisation of the cult, considering that Hermes is usually placed as a substitute for the oriental Attis.[408] It is also noticeable that an older, bearded figure, most likely of Thracian-Phrygian origin often accompanies the Great Mother and the Corybantes in depictions with mystery connotations. The curtain or *parapetasma* behind which the Curetes and the Corybantes are placed alludes without doubt to the secrecy of the ritual. Hermes taking the role of the ψυχοπομπός (Underworld soul-guide) leads the initiates into the ritual death, therefore he is sometimes also placed behind the curtain, while Hecate lights their way into the Underworld. It is a part of the ritual that was not to be revealed to those who were not participants of the mysteries. It is an allusion to *katabasis* or ritual descent into the Underworld, and the return, after which the initiate is introduced to the domain of death. Such placement of warriors within the iconography of the cult may allude to the age of the initiate – young men ready for army service.

In order to perceive the relation between the Great Goddess and the Corybantes better, we need to rely on the dynamics of the interaction of the cult and the similar spiritual systems of the antique world, and, besides the iconographical, to consider the mythological and ritual parallels. Within the context of the Mother Goddess religion, the image of the warrior can be perceived through several different perspectives; as an episode in the etiological myths; as part of a tradition of male groups centrered around figures of Great Goddesses; and as bearers of certain mystery rituals of initiation-ecstatic character.

Warriors as an episode in Greek etiological myths

As the cults are composed out of different structural elements, so are the myths made out of smaller episodes interlaced with several mythological contexts. As a result, one can explain, in a most picturesque way, the spread of a ritual and the way it was practised.[409] Etiological myths, as well as the festivals created around the Great Mother of the Gods, contain the motif of warriors, often as a reflection of magic belief. Aetiology is inseparable from the cultic places were the legend was created. The legend was revived every year; the magic was awakened, transmitting the divine power. In classical Greece, there were two ancient festivals honouring the Great Mother, richly illustrated with myths: the spring Galaxia and summer Kronia. Certain dances involving arms were performed as a typical means of celebrating the Goddess.[410]

The corresponding etiological myth to the festival of Galaxia is the one linked to the birth of Zeus. The Curetes may be directly associated with the Phrygian Corybantes in this Greek myth, transferred to Cybele when she was identified with Rea, the Greek Great Mother. It is known that the etiological myths are created in the regions where a ritual was performed and that they went through long processes of formation and assimilation with religious ideas of different spiritual systems. This legend is, above all, connected to Crete where the Couretes were of special meaning. They guarded the cave where Rea hid little Zeus from Kronos and suffocated his cry by banging their swords on their shields.[411] They even acquired the epithet *kourotrophoi* owing to their function of protectors

---

[406] Vermaseren 1978, n° 268; Musso 1983.
[407] Vermaseren 1986, n° 465.
[408] Sfameni Gasparro 1985, 73-4.

[409] Robertson 2003, 220.
[410] Robertson 1996, 241.
[411] Hesiod, *Theog.* 477-485.

of children.[412] It is believed that they founded the city of Knossos and the local temple dedicated to the Goddess (*Diod.* 5.66.1). Several locations on Crete are associated with the legend;[413] however it is traditionally assumed that Mont Ida was the place where the myth originated and spread. A cave was discovered on the northern flank of this Cretan mountain with a cache of votive objects, including over sixty shields. It is a strong indication that the ritual of the armed dancers was performed here, honouring the Great Mother worshipped even before Idaian Zeus.[414] Here, Zeus was celebrated as a vegetation deity; his cult was of initiatory nature, and, in addition to its being considered a Minoan legacy, it is also believed that it originates from Anatolia where this category of gods comes from. Caves usually served as secret chambers during the ritual of initiation and there are several on Mount Ida where the ritual of the armed warriors could have taken place.[415]

Rituals were carried further from their original sites, so the myths followed their spread and alternated according to the local sacred places and traditions. In such manner the myth of the birth of Zeus became attributed to etiological myths of other Greek sites where the Great Goddess was celebrated. Pausanius wrote about the local legend from Arcadia and revealed the existence of numerous sacred mythological places connected to the local sanctuaries of the Great Mother. Rea gave birth to Zeus in the Arcadian mountains – Mt Taumasius in the vicinity of the Metidrius – and, guarded by armed giants, showed a rock instead of a child to Kronos (Paus. 8.36.2-3). The nymphs bathed the child and watched over it together with the Curetes on the Mt Ithome (Paus. 4.33.1) near Mesena were, besides the statue of the Goddess, the work of Damophon, a *megaron* existed dedicated to the Curetes (Paus. 4.31.6, 9). Pausanius (8.30.4) further writes that there was also a damaged temple in Megalopolis and a sanctuary dedicated to Despoina near Lycosura (8.37.2).[416] Among the fragments of relief depictions of the celebrated statue of Damophon, tympana and lions, groups of armed warriors were also found, again an indication of the local rite with ecstatic armed dances.[417] We also find the figures of the Couretes on the base of a terracotta figurine from Tegeia, where Attis is depicted sitting in his usual mourning posture (fig. 138).[418] On the Athenian hill of the Muses another local tale was told about the birth of Zeus, attributed to Museius. In his Theogony, this legendary Greek poet, student of Orpheus, said that Rea gave the child Zeus to Themis, who gave it to Amaltea, who took it to the cave in Crete to be kept by a goat.[419] Although the Curetes are not mentioned in the legend, they are found in the Athenian iconography. On a fragmentary relief from the Acropolis, besides a seated Cybele with the usual attributes, the lion, the tympanum and the patera, two figures armed with shields are recognised – the Curetes.[420]

Another feature of the Mother Goddess cult present in the festivals of Galaxia is Θρόνωσις, or setting thrones for the service of the ritual that preceded the act of initiation. The initiate was placed on one of these thrones, while the other participants, already initiated, danced around him in a wild rhythm. This purifying ritual had a cathartic effect on the mystes.[421] It is the corybantic ritual that had a cleansing character or κάθαρσις.[422] On the Athenian hill of the Muses multiple ritual thrones carved in the rocks were found, made for the rituals. There are seven of them, one next to the other, divided by arm rests.[423] Θρόνωσις is a common phenomenon in the Mother Goddess cult and it is documented in other regions of the Greek world.[424] There is a similar example in Phoceia, where at least a hundred of these niches are known, divided in several groups;[425] they are also found at Ephesus[426] and on the island of Samos, where there are also groups of niches with reliefs carved in the rocks around several sanctuaries.[427] On some of them a relief figure of the Great Mother is depicted.

This fashion of celebrating the Great Mother reached the western borders of the antique world. According to Sfameni Gasparro, its appearance in Sicily, in the city of Acrai, is a phenomenon that synthesised several different ways of signifying the Mother Goddess religion. The cult came to these regions in an already syncretized form. In fact, the Great Goddess came to Sicily with the Ionians from Colophon during their colonisation of the West. On the rocks of the place today known as Colle Orbo, twelve reliefs of the Great Mother and her companions placed in a naiskos were carved (fig. 139).[428] Most of them show the Corybantes beside, or around, the Goddess's head crowned with a *polos* (fig. 140).[429] On one of them Cybele is shown in a standing posture, holding hands with the figures beside her; on her right side is Hermes with a caduceus in his left hand, while on her left is a figure with a pedum, considered to be Attis, and next to him is Hecate with a torch. The whole composition is flanked with the Dioskouroi on horses (fig. 141).[430] The ceremony of double thrones was performed in Piraeus too, where the double image of the divine Mother can be seen in the local iconography.[431] Together with Cybele, the Corybantes were also known, as well as the Phrygian mysteries. Multiplying the divine image is often seen in

---

[412] Hadzisteliou Price 1978, 193.
[413] Mount Dicte where the Dictaean Zeus was worshipped, as written on the linear B tablets from Knossos (Robertson 1996, 246-250); as well as the sanctuary in Lyctos mentioned by Hesiod (*Theog.* 192-200).
[414] Robertson 1996, 248, 252.
[415] Nilsson 1963, 31; Robertson 1996, 251.
[416] For the cult in Arcadia, see Graillot 1912, 509-11; Vermaseren 1982, n° 486-491; Robertson 1996, 254.
[417] Robertson 1996, 254.
[418] Vermaseren 1966, 9; Vermaseren 1982, n° 488.
[419] Robertson 1996, 255-257.

[420] Vermaseren 1982, n° 190.
[421] Robertson 2003, 222.
[422] Burkert 1987, 19, n. 39.
[423] Robertson 1996, 259.
[424] Clinton 2003, 63-64.
[425] Naumann 1983, 153-155.
[426] Vermaseren 1987, n° 184-189; Naumann 1983, 346-349.
[427] Naumann 1983, 217.
[428] Sfameni Gasparro 2003, 51-86.
[429] Vermaseren 1978, n° 152-164.
[430] Vermaseren 1978, n° 154.
[431] Naumann 1983, 153 – 155, 214-217; Robertson 1996, 260.

the Mother Goddess iconography; in fact, the Corybantes themselves are a multiplied depiction of a warrior.[432]

The ritual of the armed dancers was also held during the Pan-Hellenic summer festival – Kronia. Frenetic dances was performed, the worshippers shouted and followed the wild rhythm of tympana and cymbals; it was the way to evoke the Great Mother.[433] In earlier times Kronos probably had a certain significance in these festivities, although his role was more mythological than ritualistic in nature. He was considered to be a personification of the antiquity of this festival.[434] Etiological myths corresponding to Kronia are connected to other warrior groups from Greek mythology. The genealogical legend known in Olympia tells us about Pelops and the band of warriors he led from Phrygia and Lydia to the Peloponnesus. It could also indicate one of the migration routes of the ritual from Asia Minor to Greece. Pelops and his warriors came from the Mount Sypilus, a very important place in the cult of Cybele ever since the Hittite rule and from where they brought the ritual in its authentic form.[435] Pausanias (6.22.1) wrote about a temple in Olympia dedicated to Artemis Kordaka where Pelops and his followers performed the warrior dance *kordax*, similar to the ritual of the armed dancers from the Mother Goddess cult. The Corybantes had their cult in Eretria, confirmed by local inscriptions. The mythological founders of the local ritual were the conquering warriors lead by Knopus the Ionian. According to the legend, Eretria was seized with the help of a Thessalian witch who chose the strongest and biggest bull from the herd, gave him a hallucinogenic potion that caused madness and sent him to the defenders. The soldiers of Eretria, seeing a convenient opportunity and interpreting the gift as a divine sign, sacrificed the bull and feasted on the poisonous meat. After a while they began a wild and uncontrollable dance, a chance for Knopus to kill them and triumph over their city.[436]

Cyzicus, a colony of Miletus in the Propontis and one of the main centres of the cult of Cybele is associated with the myth of one of the most famous warrior bands in Greek mythology – the Argonauts. The Goddess was here known as *Kotiana, Lobrina, Plakiana*,[437] but certainly her most famous epithet was *Dindimena*, developed through the usual way of identifying the Goddess with mountains. In the vicinity of Cyzicus is Mount Dindymus on which peak a sanctuary devoted to Cybele was found.[438] It was believed that the Argonauts came to Cyzicus, build this temple dedicated to the Mother and set the ritual celebrations in her honour. According to Apollonius of Rhodes (1.935-1077), Jason and the Argonauts killed the Doliones, six armed sons of the Earth Mother. The Goddess, offended by this act, sent the Etesian winds and prevented the onward journey of Argos. To appease the Goddess the Argonauts erected her statue and began worshipping her on the peak of Mount Dindymus. They danced and shouted, producing a deep chthonic sound by banging their bronze swords against their shields. Cybele was celebrated in exactly the same way in Cyzicus during the Etesian winds. A *xoanon* of the Goddess was placed in front of the altar and a libation sacrifice was offered; the young men danced and banged their shields in the same way as the legendary Argonauts had, while the other participants played the rhombus and the tympana (*Apoll. Rhod.* 1.1103-1152).[439] We also know about the ritual in Cyzicus from Herodotus (4. 76. 2-5) in the legend of the Anacharsis the Scythian who came to this city during his journeys. Here he sacrificed to the Goddess in order to ensure a safe trip to his homeland across the dangerous seas. He took a vow to continue celebrating the Goddess in his country in the same way in which he was initiated – with the nocturnal ceremony παννυχίς and the sound of tympana, in the thick mountain woods. He failed; the ritual was not accepted and for that reason he was killed. On the relief considered to be from Cyzicus, now in the British museum (fig. 142),[440] Cybele is depicted on a throne with a patera and a sceptre. There are standing figures of a bearded god and Hermes in front of her, while in the back there are two warriors with smaller dimensions, armed with shields and swords. On the opposite upper corner a ship is shown and a person sitting on a rock, probably a depiction of the reason this ritual was created – to abate the force of nature over which the Goddess reigns. It is considered that the Corybantes and the Couretes are the prototypes of the armed dancers in the cult of the Great Mother, who perform the ritual warrior dance (□νόπλιος όρχσις) at the Kronia festival. In Cyzicus, the mythological ancestors of the ritual were the Argonauts.[441]

The Corybantes: male groups, companions of the Great Mother, and supporters of the mystery ritual

The Corybantes belong to the so called 'Societies of Gods', strictly determined according to sex and age. They are the companions of the Olympian Gods, although most commonly grouped around the figure of the Great Mother. These societies are in fact mythological prototypes of the exclusive cult associations (*thiasoi*), often organised for practising mysteries.[442] On this basis, as well as by their mystery and soteriological characteristics, the Corybantes and the Curetes are connected to other 'Societies of Gods'.

A group of gods belonging to these societies are the Dactyls, healer gods and traditional companions of the Great Mother, also identified with the Corybantes and the Curetes. They are a personification of the fraternity of

---

[432] More about this phenomenon Hadzisteliou Price 1971, 48-69.
[433] Robertson believes that the Great Mother was the only deity worshipped in this fashion and that the name of the festival derived from *kernea* (1996, 281-286).
[434] Versnel 1987, 128.
[435] Robertson 1996, 296-297.
[436] Burkert 1979, 59-60.
[437] Schwertheim 1976, 809-815.
[438] Rein 1996, 229.
[439] Summers 1996, 350.
[440] Vermaseren 1977b, 69.
[441] Robertson 1996, 292-293.
[442] Burkert 1977, 173-4.

metallurgical craftsmen, therefore identified also with the Kabiri. It is believed that the Dactyls constituted the mysteries of Samothrace and that they taught these rites to Orpheus so that he might spread them among men.[443] Ephorus (FGrH 70 F 104), among other things, speaks of the Dactyls as wizards who practised magic. According to the traditional Eleian legend, Rea gave the infant Zeus to the Dactyls to keep him safe. Pausanius (5.7.6.-7,9,14.7), on the other hand, wrote that the Dactyls were sent to Olympia from the Cretan Mount Ida, yet their epithet 'Idean' does not have a topographical but etymological background, signifying them as 'beings from the woods' (the epithet comes from the noun ίδε (wood)). This is, in fact, the etiological myth of the summer festivals in Olympia where a Metroon existed in the fourth century B.C. In the deposits of this temple, among the others votive objects, bronze cymbals were found, clear indication of the practice of the particular ritual.[444]

The Dioskouroi can be recognised on several Mother Goddess monuments, as we have already seen on the rocks of Sicily and the relief from Lebadeia. They became part of the iconography of Cybele by syncretizing with the Curetes and the Corybantes, despite the fact that there is no definite mythological connection between them. They are often placed in the mystery environment and, with Dionysius and Heracles, are well known initiates depicted in the classic iconography of the Eleusinian mysteries.[445] The divine twins are most often connected with Cybele in Roman times, especially in the provinces.[446] They are also known as soteriologycal gods and as protectors during sea travels.[447]

The need to please the gods in order to ensure safe sailing leads us towards Samothrace, the Great Gods, and their mystery rituals. The Argonauts, before they established the ritual in Cyzicus, were themselves initiated in the mysteries of the Great Gods from Samothrace. The necessity for divine intervention comes from the geographical position of this island on the dangerous route from the Aegean to the Propontis.[448] One of the characteristics of the mysteries from Samothrace is the already described Corybantic ritual of *thronosis*. The Great Gods from Samothrace are identified with the Corybantes by several ancient authors. For example, Diodorus (3.55.9) tells us about the Great Mother and her sons, the Corybantes that brought the mysteries to this island; the name of their father was not to be spoken and was revealed only during the initiations.[449] On Samothrace, judging by the iconography, the Great Goddess can be identified with Cybele, while the young god Kadmilos with Hermes.[450]

In this context, however, we should pay more attention to the Thraco-Phrygian cult of the Kabiri, in many ways similar to the cult of Cybele. The Kabiri are gods of fire and metallurgy, sons of Hephaestus and the personification of secret, mystery societies, formed around the Great Goddess. Together with Dionysus, Hermes, and the Great Goddess, they are considered as royal divinities, very important in the initiation rituals of the aristocracy. The Macedonian dynasty was especially fond of the cult of the Kabiri and practised their mystery rites.[451] The mysteries of the Kabiri are close to the Eleusinian and are of initiatory character – a ritual descent in the Underworld, or the *katabasis*, was performed. These gods were considered second-rank gods or daemons and were identified with the Corybantes, Couretes, and the Telchines.[452] Usually, there are three, but sometimes a fourth god is also added – Kadmos or the ithyphallic Hermes, as named by Herodotus (2.51). There were three Kabiri and three Kabiric nymphs known at Lemnos, gravitating around Hephaestus from the very early periods. They came to Thebes during the migrations in the eighth and the seventh century B.C. In the local Theban myth two Kabiri are mentioned and added to the Dionysian mythological cycle, as well as to the myths of Pan and Hermes.[453]

The Dionysian rituals served the cult greatly, not only, for example, while formulating the Hellenised rituals of Cybele, but also by assisting the Goddess in the process of naturalisation in the Greek world. Euripides in his description of the Corybantes touched on this connection in a wonderful way:

> *O grottos of the Couretes, and the godly Cretan*
> *Zeus's progenitors the woodlands! there, triple-crested in caverns,*
> *circlements strung with leather (such as mine)*
> *Corybants discover'd,*
> *bacchanti sing and highly-strung*
> *whistlings mingling in, Phrygian woodwinds*
> *sweet in their crying, and to mother Rhea gave*
> *it, banging to Bacchic*
> *evoiing:...*[454]

The Corybantes and Cybele are connected with Dionysus on the ritual as well as mythological level. They are the guardians of the little Dionysus in a tale known to us

---

[443] Bonnechere 2003, 171.
[444] Robertson 1996, 298.
[445] Bonnechere 2003, 170.
[446] On the relief from Cotyaeum Cybele is flanked by the Dioskouroi and accompanied by the figures of Luna, Sol and the Thracian rider (Vermaseren 1987, n° 139); The statue of a standing Cybele between lions from Brindisi is placed on a base whose front is decorated with the Dioskouri on horses (Vermaseren 1987, n° 122). Finds of the images of the Dioskouri together with Cybele are also known from Germania. It is supposed that on the kantharos from Stevensweert from the first half of the first century, among six heads of divinities, there is also the head of Cybele, placed between the Dioskouri (Vermaseren 1989, n° 12). On the second-century relief from Marbach, the central figure is Mercury, surrounded by eleven divinities. The first figure on his left side is Cybele with *corona muralis*, on a throne, with a lion on her lap. In the lower part, there are the Dioskouri with horses between Mars and Hercules (Vermaseren 1989, n° 61). The Dioskouri within the context of the Mother Goddess religion were depicted on the frescoes of the Roman Hypogeum (Vermaseren, 1977a, 55-6).
[447] Brelich 1963, 39.
[448] Bonnechere 2003, 171.

[449] Clinton 2003, 64.
[450] Burkert 1977, 283.
[451] Маразов 1992, 151-152.
[452] Маразов 1994, 83-84.
[453] Schachter 2003, 112.
[454] *Bacch.* 120-31. Trans. M. A. Neuburg.

from later times, transmitted by the poet Nonnus in the fifth century (*Dionysiaca* 9.160). According to this legend, Rea took the young god in Phrygia where the Corybantes guarded him. Dionysus grew with their music and dance, just as his father Zeus did on Crete. So, the Corybantes are common element in the mythology of both Cybele and Dionysus. Their rituals are very similar in character as well, especially in the ecstatic moment produced by music, and during which one comes closer to 'the divine'. The celebrations of Cybele and Dionysus, with ecstatic music and wild dance, were followed by a period of frenzy as a sign of divine presence.

We have noticed that the Corybantes are linked with many mystery aspects of the cult of Cybele. They follow the healing aspect of the Goddess, as well as the cathartic – orgiastic one in relation to the ritual musical instruments. The identification of some of the elements of Corybantism with the Mother Goddess ones, as well as with the Dionysian cult, comes from the state of the divine possession gained during their rituals.[455] In the Pessinuntian myth the Goddess punished Attis with madness because of his infidelity, as a result of which he castrated himself under a pine tree.[456] Likewise, the Corybantes shared the power to inflict mental disorder and to liberate from it.[457] As well as coming from Cybele and the Corybantes, this kind of madness (*mania*) was also sent by Pan, Poseidon, and Hecate, as well as by all the heroes who descended to the Underworld.[458] *Mania* is a condition of madness and emotional exaltation followed by a wild pounding of the heart and irrational fear which Cybele sends to people as a result of their impiety. It is a state of unhealthy mind and spirit accompanied sometimes by actual physical symptoms. This condition is also known as corybantic illness or κορυβαντισμός. *Mania* was exorcised by practising the rituals of Corybantism in order to return to a state of sanity and peace. It was made in a homeopathic way – *mania* is to be cured by means of *mania*. The inner anxiety was suppressed by an external factor; a simulation of personal madness achieved through ecstatic and wild dancing. After this intensive and cathartic ritual, an indescribable collective peace and spiritual satisfaction followed. The ritual of the Corybantes was described in several Athenian dramas. However we get most of our details about the practice and meaning of Corybantism in classical Greece from Plato.[459]

Linforth tried to reconstruct the ritual by analyzing six works of this philosopher, who was highly affirmative of Corybantism: a group rhythmic activity, with accentuated healing characteristics and an emphasis on direct personal gain, while celebrating the gods was only secondary. Sacrificing preceded the ritual, and it is not certain whether it was group or individual, but if accompanied by positive signs, it had a curative result. The palliative effect of Corybantism drew participants (κορυβαντιῶντες) to a periodic repetition of the ritual, which in a way made them dependent and emotionally unstable.[460] Apart from the obvious similarities with the mystery cults, Corybantism had a separate development and distinctive features. The armed dance was not part of it and the tympana were not played; instead the sound of flutes (*tibiae*) was used. The fundamental difference was that Corybantism was not of a secret character, moreover, it was completely accepted within all classes of society and it enriched the Greek language with several common phrases.[461]

The ritual belongs to the group of Greek *theletai*, mystery initiation rituals to do with adulthood or rites of maturity. In this sense, the Corybantes and their respective figures in the Mother Goddess iconography may point to the age group of the initiates in this ritual – predominantly young men ready to go to war. The age equivalent of women initiates would be their readiness for sexual activity. *Theletai* has been spoken of in connection with the mysteries in Samothrace, with Dionysian rituals, and with those devoted to Cybele, accentuating the therapeutic effect, but also the practical aspect of heeling – as they mentioned in connection with the Eleusinian mysteries. Burkert finds an analogy with the Egyptian healing magic. However, he considers that the magic in Egypt was used while heeling an actual illness, and not to fill the practitioner with divine grace as as the case with the Greek mysteries.[462]

We find another phenomenon, close to the Corybantism, this time in Ephesus and associated with the Couretes. Here, in Hellenistic time a holy college of the Couretes existed, renewed during the reign of Commodes. This fraternity belonged to the Ephesian ruling class and was supervised by the prytaneum, the political and religious centre. Together with the mysteries devoted to Artemis, the mysteries of the Couretes were also recognised, moreover, they were legally accepted and during which young boys were initiated, practising the ritual of the warriors.[463]

The Corybantes in Rome and the eastern influences on the cult in Iader

The Corybantes, alongside Cybele were known in Rome in the late Republic, even before the acceptance of Attis. A serial of coins was minted in 78 B.C. commemorating the five most important Roman games (*ludi Romani, Plebeii, Cereales, Apollinares* and *Megalenses*) with singular depictions of Jupiter, Hercules, Liber with Ceres, Apollo, and Cybele. The image of crowned Cybele appears on a throne and in a chariot drawn by lions. She holds the reins herself as well as her usual attribute - the patera. On the obverse of one of these coins is an image

---

[455] Dodds 1956, 77-79.
[456] The legend is transmitted through Thimoteus. Pausanias (7, 17, 10-12) and Arnobius (*Adv. Nat.* 5, 5-7) refer to th latter.
[457] Pind. *Pyth.* 3.137id; Diog. Trag. 1.5, p. 776 N²; Diod. 3.58.2.
[458] Eur. *Hipp.* 141id; compare Dodds 1956, 77.
[459] Linforth 1946, 121-162.

[460] Linforth 1946, 133-134.
[461] Linforth 1946, 156.
[462] Burkert 1987a, 18-21.
[463] Graff 2003, 241-51.

of a Corybant,[464] which could lead us to an assumption that the ecstatic armed dance was well known during the early acceptance of the Mother Goddess religion and was part of the *ludi Megalenses*.

The Corybantes, as well as the description of the ritual, are to be found in the Roman literature of the late Republican period. Lucretius in *De rerum natura* (600-60) writes about the participants in the *pompa* who play instruments, wave their knives, bloody from castration, and shake the plumes of their helmets. Besides the general opinion that Lucretius described Greek rituals, Summers believes that in this case the author referred to a Roman procession as part of the festival Megalensia. Among the usual instruments such as tympana, cymbals and tibiae used during the procession, Lucretius also mentions horns (*raucisonoque minantur cornua cantu*) (6.619), a novelty in Roman Mother Goddess rituals. It is in fact an Etruscan instrument that was adopted by the Romans and used not only in their war campaigns and athletic games, but also during the ecstatic celebrations honouring the gods.[465] Diogenes (TrGF 45 F1.3) also makes notice of the same instruments, but adds the *rhombus*, an instrument used in Greek initiation rituals. According to Apollonius of Rhodes (1.1138-39), the Argonauts taught the local Phrygian population how to use the rhombus in the celebrations of Cybele.

Judging by the *Ara Pietatis Augustae* (fig. 143), the Corybantes featured on part of the architectural decoration of the Metroon on the Palatine. On the relief we see the front of the temple after its restoration. The Goddess is symbolically depicted on the pediment with a *corona muralis* placed on a throne and flanked by two reclining figures with tympana and two lions. A figure of a Corybant with a shield and lance is shown as the right-hand *acroterium* of the pediment.[466] On the base of a monument from Sorrento erected in honour of Augustus a dancing Corybant is also depicted together with Cybele.[467] The only single statue so far known of a Corybant (fig. 144) is again in connection with the Mother Goddess religion. It was found within the *Campus Magnae Matris* in Ostia, on the east side where there was an *Attideum* decorated with marble Pan statues. It is from the second century and it bears a dedication made by Caius Cartilius Euplus.[468]

The ritual of the armed warriors is present in the March festivals honouring Attis. On the day *arbour intrat* commemorated on March 22 the *dendrophoroi* carried a decorated pine tree symbolizing Attis into the temple. The next day the *Salii*, priests of Mars, danced in a procession on the streets of Rome, in a similar fashion as the Corybantes did, playing the trumpets and banging their shields.[469] It is possible that this older ritual additionally influenced the acceptance of the Great Mother in Rome. It is worth noticing that rudiments of the ritual of the Corybantes were maintained during the Middle Ages. Tarantism, or the religion of 'guilty conscience' held in summer, had a therapeutic effect and the effect of group healing session, the same as the Corybantism. It ensured instant relief and was of especial help to women in their hysterical moments. This ritual spread to Germany, Holland and Belgium in the 15th century. One can still meet people practising Tarantism in the secluded villages of northern Italy.[470]

Although the cult in Dalmatia was venerated during Romanisation, eastern influences also acted upon its development, coming from the Danube provinces, or with the orientals.[471] In an atmosphere open towards eastern spiritual ideas, and in parallel with the official way of celebrating the Great Goddess, there existed rituals of mystery-initiating character, directly connected to the Phrygian practice. Iconographical evidence of these rituals is known from the sites where the mysteries of Cybele were held. Up to now, the belief was that mysteries in *Iader* developed by way of a diffusion of the cults of Mithra and Sabazius,[472] while the fresco additionally reflects the connection with the Dionysian and the Kabiric mysteries, as well as the fact that the local wealthy population was inclined to their practice.

The warrior on the fresco from *Iader* directs us to the idea that the initiatory armed dance ritual was known within the structural frame of the local cult. A similar rite could have existed even before the acceptance of Cybele, which was naturally adopted and adapted in her cult. We know of a warrior dance in northeast Albania and Kosovo originating from south Illyria from pre-Roman times, and even performed to this day. The dance is the same as the one of the mythological Corybantes; following the rhythm of drums and the sound of clashing weapons.[473] Furthermore, the chamber itself where the fresco was found (considered as an underground sanctuary and simultaneously serving as Spelaeum, Serapeum and Metroon[474]) leads us to thought that the initiation ritual of *katabasis* was performed here. Underground chambers were often used while performing mystery rituals, especially in the Kabiric mysteries.[475] In accordance with the different local conceptions of the Kabiri, we lack a specific iconography of these gods. However, usually there is a bearded god in connection with them, whose name written on a fifth-century vase is Kabeiros.[476] A hierogamy between the Great Goddess and the Kabiric Great God is shown on the friezes from the Borovo rhython. There are some recognizable Dionysian orgiastic elements as well.[477] We have seen that on the fourth-

---

[464] Summers 1996, 344; Turcan 1996b, 39.
[465] Summers 1996, 361.
[466] Vermaseren 1977a, 42-43; Vermaseren 1977c, n° 2.
[467] Vermaseren 1997a, 81; Vermaseren 1978, n° 76.
[468] Vermaseren 1977a, 60-62; Vermaseren 1977c, n°377.
[469] Vermaseren 1977a, 115.

[470] Lewis 1971, 41f.
[471] Turcan 1996, 65.
[472] Suić 1965b, 116.
[473] Sako 1972, 307-310; Stipčević 1974, 231-2.
[474] Medini 1993, 8.
[475] Маразов 1992, 149.
[476] Маразов 1992, 124.
[477] Between the figures of satyrs and maenads, there is a depiction of a man and a woman in an embrace (Маразов 1992, 136-7). According to the descriptions of Suić and Medini an embracing couple was also depicted on the fresco from Zadar.

century reliefs from Piraeus, Amphipolis and Lebadea, together with the Goddess, there is a bearded god, who is also present on the fresco from *Iader*. The meaning of the bearded god within the iconography of Cybele is undoubtedly mysterious, bearing in mind that the monuments on which he appears have mystery connotations. Another common element is the symbolic depiction of *katabasis*, also present on the relief dedicated to Bendis. However, the bearded god is not present on other monuments where Cybele is shown together with the Corybantes, which leads us to the assumption that in southeast Thracia and on the nearby islands, as well as in Macedonia, the cult of Cybele was syncretized with the one of the Kabiri. There is a similar example on the *Iader* fresco, only it is not certain whether a curtain was also depicted here. Interiors with mosaics and wall decorations are usually associated with mystery and hero cults, as for example the west sanctuary at Samothrace.[478] It is highly possible that the Kabiric mysteries came into contact with the ones of the Cybele in *Iader*, unless they arrived there in an already syncretized form. It is confirmed that the Kabiri were present in Pannonian *Mursa* brought with Thracian immigrants.[479] Concerning the other depicted figures, one can say a little more in addition. The *symplegma* is an indicator that the ritual in *Iader* had an orgiastic character, or that the concept of *hireos gamos* was familiar, the snake additionally alludes to the chthonic nature of the mysteries of Cybele in *Iader*, while the youth with the raised arm illustrates the spiritual enthusiasm and the catharsis present in the ritual.

According to the abundance of data, the mythological-ritual importance of the Corybantes in the cult and myth of Cybele is multi-layered, as we have, in fact, tried to portray. Above all, they allude to the ritual of the ecstatic character connected to rhythmic music and dance in the service of the initiation practise. The image of the warrior within the religious systems is usually a symbolic reflection of secret cultic organisations, or of the aristocracy protected by the Great Mother. The warrior on the fresco from Zadar must have had the same symbolism.

---

[478] Lawall 2003, 93.
[479] See Bulat 1997, 21-32.

CONCLUSION

In order to understand the basic concept of the spiritual message of the system created around the Great Mother Cybele, it is necessary to explore the development of the cult and the pertaining symbolism, and to find the common component recognisable in all the regions and through all times of its existence. It is easily conceivable that duality is expressed in almost every manifestation of the cult. Looking for the earliest symbolic image connected to this cult, we come to the culture of Çatal Hüyük and the crowned Goddess giving birth on a throne. Death was part of the life of this culture, while the Goddess was protectress of these two spheres. Her counter-balance is the male fecundity force, most often seen in the motif of the bull, either in the iconographical or in the ritual sense. The dual divine power is demonstrated in the presence of two lions surrounding the Goddess, but also in the figure of the so-called 'twins'. Later, in the myth this dual power is illustrated through the image of the androgen Agdistis, the embodiment of the male and female principal, the unstable monstrous figure capable of both creation and destruction. Although duality is recognisable in many divinities, it is certainly most present in the figure of the Great Goddess Cybele. As all Great Goddesses, she also carries within herself the elementary division of power of life and death and is capable of giving birth, but also of taking life away, of healing and also causing suffering, of enabling eternal spiritual peace and of inflicting unbearable madness. She is the protectress of both social order and the wild natural forces. Cybele is accompanied by two lions, two acolytes; her image is doubled, not only in the Athenian *naiskoi*, but already on Hittite seals. Duality is a spiritual concept present also within the territory of the Illyric, into which Cybele was added. The *Nesactium* sculpture attracts special attention, above all, the Goddess giving birth and a dual head that speaks of the local awareness of the duality concept. This cult material is comparable to that from Çatal Hüyük. Cybele met the autochthonous Liburnian goddesses of fertility such as Iria, Latra and Venus Anzotica. Bearing in mind Cybele's strong syncretistic power, it is most likely that she subsumed their cults in her own religious system. Attis is also a dual figure and it is unnecessary to emphasise additionally something which is clearly seen through the images of *Attis tristis* and *Attis hilaris*, personifications of the ritual division of the festival in March of days of mourning and joy.

The Mother Goddess cult most certainly left a deep trace in the religion of the ancient inhabitants of the territory of today's Republic of Croatia. More than 120 monuments related to this cult, including marble statues, inscriptions, bronze statuettes, appliqués, sarcophagi, tombstones, and votive lead and marble plates reveal the importance of the cult among the local population. It came here in the first century A.D. during the Romanisation of the region, brought by Roman soldiers; it gained official status and flourished in the second century, while already in the next, because of the spreading of Christianity, the decline of its popularity can be noticed. Because of the heterogeneity of the area, we cannot comprehend the cult uniformly. The Goddess adapted differently in different parts of the region. From these reasons we follow several distinct forms of the way the cult existed in Roman times on the territory of Republic of Croatia. The basic division would be that of the Dalmatian and Pannonian regions. In the area of Histria, the cult developed similarly as in Dalmatia because of the strong Italian influence. The importance of Aquileia for the development of the local cult is established, although, judging by the use of the cultic symbols, it is possible that the influence also arrived by way of the south-eastern provinces. The iconography from the province of Pannonia, which offers a rather different symbolism, leads mostly to this assumption.

The earliest centre where the cult attained official status was in *Senia*, where an existence of a Metroon was confirmed, positioned on a highly important central spot and decorated with statues of the Goddess. It is quite possible that the same happened in *Aenona*, *Arba*, and on the island of Brač, although firm archaeological proof is still lacking. The statue discovered in *Mursa* with its representative character can refer to the official status of the cult in this city as well. In *Burnum*, the cult existed within the frameworks of the imperial cult, and the Metroon was positioned on the northeast side of the Forum. The official acceptance of the cult in Dalmatia was also affirmed by the presence of the *archigallus* Lucius Demetrius Barbunteus in *Salona*. However, a central temple connected to his service was not found. Proofs of the existence of private sacral buildings are to be found on many inscriptions, most of them the legacy of the *cognationes* protected by the Great Mother. We are also aware of a Cybele's peripetal temple with hexagonal base and crypt in Diocletian's Palace. A building in service of the cult was found in *Iader* as well, but of private, not public character. It was assigned to the mystery rituals of an initiatory-esoteric kind, during which music was used in order to achieve a state of frenzy as one of the ways to learn the higher states of consciousness and spiritual change.

Mysteries were created upon the basis of agrarian cults created around Great Goddesses, so it is reasonable to think that the autochthonic tradition of chthonic cults of the Goddesses from Liburnia and Histria continued through the cult of the Great Goddess Cybele. *Salona* also draws attention to the existence of the mystery elements of the cult in the province of Dalmatia. On local statues Cybele holds the *cista mystica*, an object with a strong mystery connotation, while the firmest indicator of this notion is the inscription of Curia Prisca, where we read of liturgical instruments symbolically used in Roman mystery rituals. The soteriological aspect of Cybele in *Salona* is also accentuated. This power of the Goddess is directed towards protection of life on earth, known within the circle of the *cognationes*, whose presence was restricted only in the Salonitan area, especially in the area of the river Iadro. It is probable that the *cognationes* were of mystery character. Those organizations were likely secret and exclusive and their members practised Cybele's mysteries. Indeed, the mystery elements were preserved in private communities created around the cult. The iatric character of Cybele was particularly known in Cyzicus and Thebes, where the cult was associated with rich mythology, whose episodes are connected with the eastern coast of the Adriatic. The mythological founder of Thebes, Cadmos and his wife Harmonia, were initiated in the mysteries on Samothrace in honour of the Mother and spent their final days in these parts. Also, the Argonauts, the mythological founders of the ecstatic ritual honouring the Mother in Cyzicus, on their way back from Chalcis, passed by the Adriatic coast and stopped on the Brygean islands.

The route followed by the Goddess is traceable in the development of the cultic practice. Some of these elements are to be seen through the motif of the armed companion of Cybele, which points to a certain character of the cult and therefore it is an inevitable part of the whole portrayal of her cult. By choosing the image of the warrior as one of the ways to observe the mythological and ritual system of the Great Mother, a narrative landscape opened, leading us from Neolithic times, across Greece and Rome, and all the way to the fresco in the Zadar Forum. Mythological warriors follow the Great Mother in the episodes of the Argonauts, Curetes and Corybantes. The warrior as a symbol, contemplated in conceptual ways, points to a certain social structure of the worshippers. For example, a certain exclusivity existed among those honouring the Goddess. The practice of the cult was especially popular among the aristocracy and the ruling stratum. The warrior illustrates an ancient initiation ritual which the aristocracy accepted in their ways of honouring the Goddess. She was celebrated in a frenetic fashion with ecstatic music and dance, in Anatolia as well as in Greece, Rome, and the provinces, while rudiments of this practice can be recognized even today. The ritual of ecstatic character followed by music and dance has a tradition even among the Hittites, present in the Greek Kronia and in the processions of Megalensia and the March festivals in Rome. The warrior on the walls of the underground chamber in *Iader* tells us that the Goddess was also worshipped here among the aristocracy and the higher social class, most likely initiated through the ritual of katabasis.

There are enough signs on Croatian monuments through which we can confirm that the March festivals were also performed, perhaps, however, in a different form created by the fusion of the autochthonous tradition and Roman-Phrygian rituals. Indication of the practise of rituals of Attis after the model of Roman public festivities is the presence of the order of dendrophoroi in the provinces. They were confirmed with inscriptions from *Pola*, *Salona*, and *Siscia*, while their formation is most often connected with the March festivals. The images of *Attis tristis* and *Attis hilaris* followed by the usual symbolism, additionally speak in favour of this conclusion.

Cybele and Attis on Croatian material were found together only on the relief from *Burnum* illustrating the mythological scene of the castration of Attis. This fact, along with the fact that monuments devoted to Cybele are quite different than those devoted to Attis, leads to a conclusion that in some areas the two deities were worshipped independently from one another. Their advent was evidenced in the first century at the earliest, the time when their religious meaning in the ritual sense was already differentiated. The analysis of the finds guides us to the same conclusion. While we see Cybele as the object of the public cult to whom temples were dedicated, Attis was worshipped more individually, so his image is most often found on funerary appliqués, tombstones and sarcophagi. His name is never on votive inscriptions, or on any epigraphical find. His figure is not a direct determinant of cult worship. Maybe he can be best explained if we were to say that his image was created to serve as an example. In every religious doctrine, however contemporised, there are rudiments of primitive spiritual elements. Attis, from the beginning, offered a paradigm of a certain ritual practice through which worshippers came closer to the religiosity of the Goddess. It is certainly easier to identify with an already existing figure. Attis was above all a shepherd; he leads the worshippers along the same way he himself passed. To create a portrait of this god and to how he was locally accepted, it is necessary to place the cult in a wider social and religious context. The needs of people created the god: and his cult is an expression of their needs. Thus, it is justified to assume that the inhabitants of Dalmatia recognised in Attis the local god Silvanus. In the rural parts of Dalmatia Attis was most probably treated as a vegetation god, who, as a symbol on tombstones, was a reminder of the cyclical nature of life and nature. His later character as celestial and sun god was not understood nor needed. However, in the cities and the bigger centres of the cult, not only in Dalmatia, but also in Pannonia and Histria, Attis was conceived with deeper religious understanding, attested with his cultic symbols. In Late Antiquity, Attis conveyed a vision of heavenly immortality of soul, a religious idea of which the tomb of Aeronius Firmin in *Salona* is the best example. In Histria Attis was seen in a similar light, as in the province of Dalmatia, bearing in mind that here existed a rather different spiritual tradition. As in Liburnia, female fertility deities were also dominant, a tradition from prehistory, into which Magna Mater fitted naturally. The oriental religions, where a mystery aspect developed, spread throughout the antique West, mainly owing to their eschatological characteristics. This is also why they left a deep trace in the funeral symbolism. Looking from the eschatological perspective, Attis was also a saviour god, as confirmed from many Croatian finds.

While perceiving certain characteristics of Attis, it can be assumed that on the monuments in some regions he existed only as a symbolic figure of death and regeneration. Croatian material provides a rich material legacy where his image is recognized as a guide for souls in the Underworld (ψυχοπομπός), shown to a great extent and in various ways. However the presence of the figure of Attis meant that the ecstatic-orgiastic elements of the cult were also present. Mystery religions were not closed systems; moreover, between them there was a diffusion of ideas and symbols recognisable in Attis's iconography, in the decorative elements of Dionysian religion, or in the influence of the cult of the Kabiri and Sabazius. The key to revealing the rituality of cults lies exactly in their symbols and allegorical depictions, which, beginning in Hellenistic times, became the language of spiritual systems, especially those of a mystery character, offering the worshippers images instead of words.

The cult in the regions of Illyricum follows a distinctive autochthonous development upon which different influences acted, coming from the West and East. By coupling these two influences a unique form for the worship of Cybele and Attis was created as distinct from other parts of the Roman Empire. However, two distinctions of the cultic imagery can be differentiated – Pannonian and Dalmatian. Besides common elements such as the time of the acceptance, the official form of the cult, and the presence of the dendrophoroi – a result of Italic influence, as well as the possible practise of *criobolius* – we are also able to perceive the differences. In-depth study of all occurring forms of the Mother Goddess cult, and in particular the cult iconography, leads to a conclusion that its development in Illyric was largely affected by oriental influences, particularly emphasized in the Pannonian area. Being placed on the conjunction of eastern and western cultural influence, this area unites several cultic images. A rather specific mixture of eastern and western symbols developed, collected in order to express the religiosity of the local population. We notice that the cult of the Kabiri, or to be more precise, the Kabiric type of divinities, greatly acted upon the development of the cult in this province: an influence which can also be seen in the mystery iconography of the Mother Goddess cult in the province of Dalmatia, particularly on the fresco from Zadar. This is the Thracian influence which acted upon the forming of the cult even during later, Roman times. The Mother Goddess cult syncretized with the cult of the Kabiri and as such came to the Pannonia, but also to Dalmatia.

CATALOGUE

I DALMATIA:

I. 1. *TARSATICA* (modern Rijeka)

I. 1.1. Stone sculpture of mourning Attis with crossed legs. According to J. Medini, this sculpture is not of Liburnian origin. It was part of the collection of the Count of Nugent and was mostly collected in Italy. It was kept in the Castle of Trsat and was bought by the Archaeological Museum in Zagreb.

Literature: Graillot 1912, 491; Medini 1993, 2.

I. 2. *SENIA* (modern Senj)

I. 2. 1. Metroon discovered during archaeological research in 1949-50 under the altar of the Cathedral with remains of an antique house with a triclinium and parts of the atrium. The house is connected to the reddish marble walls of the Metroon. They were razed to the ground in a fire in the fourth century. (fig. 10)

Date: end of the first or the beginning of second until the fourth century A. D.

Literature: Degmedžić 1952, 251-262; Glavičić 1968, 22; Medini 1978, 734f; Medini 1981b, n° 2; Vermaseren, 1989, n° 127.

I. 2. 2. Two fragments of a white marble *epistylium* with an inscription in a frame (*tabula ansata*). (fig. 9)

M(agnae) d(eorum) M(atri) Aug(ustae) sa[c(rum)] / Verridia Psych[e] d(e) s(ua) p(ecunia) f(ecit).

Archaeological Lapidarium of the City Museum in Senj.

Date: middle of the second century A. D.

Literature: Degmedžić 1952, 251-4, fig 1, 3; Medini 1978, pl. 148, fig. 2; Medini 1981b, n° 3; Vermaseren 1989, 128.

I. 2. 3. Fragmented white marble sculpture of Cybele discovered in three pieces. The Goddess is sitting on a throne with a back-rest and arm-rests. She is dressed in a high-girdled chiton and himation, with sandals on her feet. There are lions sitting by her legs; the left one is missing the head and most of the body. The statue was discovered close to the altar of the Cathedral in a secondary use, built in a medieval wall. (fig. 23)

Archaeological Lapidarium of the Museum of Senj.

Dimensions: height 0.940 m.

Date: end of the first-middle of the second century A. D.

Literature: SZ 3 (1967-8), 20; Medini 1978, 737–739, pl. 149–151; Medini 1981b, n° 5; Vermaseren 1989, n° 129; Cambi 2005b, 123, fig. 184.

I. 2. 4. Fine-grain white marble sculpture of Cybele. The Goddess is sitting on a rock. She is dressed in a chiton and himation with its hem over her knees; she is wearing sandals on her feet. The legs are parted with the left one extended forward. There are three animals on each side. On the right side there is a bull with a sheep under it, and a lion's head in front of them. On the left one there is a bull, with a ram's head with large horns under it. It is assumed that here there was a lion as well, but the statue is ruined. The statue was discovered 30 meters away from the previous statue. (fig. 24)

Archaeological Lapidarium of the Museum of Senj.

Date: end of the first-middle of second century A. D.

Literature: SZ 3 (1967-8), 20; Degmedžić 1952, 252-4; Glavičić 1968, 20f; Medini 1978, 734–736, pl. 143, 147; Medini 1981b, n° 4; Vermaseren 1989, n° 130; Cambi 2005b, 123-124, fig. 185.

I. 2. 5. Marble head of a Goddess. The hair is fashioned in a *crobylos*. Eyes wide open without pupils. Discovered in secondary use in a medieval wall. (figs. 25, 26)

Archaeological Museum in Zagreb.

Dimensions: height 0.165 m.

Date: first century-middle of second century A. D.

Literature: Degmeđić 1952, 254, fig. 4; Medini 1978, 736, n.11, pl. 148, I; Medini 1981b, n° 6.

I. 3. *ARBA* (modern Rab)

I. 3. 1. Inscription recorded in a medieval codex.

> *Matri Deum*
> *porticus in me-*
> *moriam suorum*
> *T(itus) Prusius T(iti) f(ilius) Ser(gia tribu) Optatus*
> 5 *p(oni) iussit per Babriam T(iti) F(iliam) Tertullam*
> *sororem heredemque.*

Lost.

Date: first century-beginning of second century A. D.

Literature: CIL III 3115; Graillot 1912, n.1; Medini 1967, 48; Medini 1978, 733–734; Schillinger 1978, 55-56, 66f; Medini 1981b, n°1; Vermaseren 1989, n° 131.

I. 4. *AENONA* (modern Nin)

I. 4. 1. White marble Attis head wearing a Phrygian cap. The exact location of discovery is unknown. It belonged to the Danielli-Pelegrini collection, and it was later kept in the Seminarium of Udine.

Current location is unknown.

Dimensions: height 0.220 m, thickness 0.185 m, width 0.190 m.

Literature: Bankò, Sticotti 1896, 151-152, n° 111; Graillot 1912, 491 n. 1; Medini 1978, 741; Medini 1981b, n° 7; Vermaseren 1989, n° 132.

1. 4. 2. Bronze cast appliqué shaped as the front of Attis's head, probably a find from a necropolis. Attis wears a Phrygian cap on the head with parallel rows of small holes. The reverse hollow space is filled with lead. The object used for connecting is visible on the reverse. High quality production. (fig. 78)

Archaeological Museum in Zagreb. Inv. No. 4763.

Dimensions: height 0.027 m, width 0.023 mm.

Date: second-third century A. D.

Literature: Medini 1968, 155, n° 11, T. IV; Medini 1977, 200-201; Medini 1978, 741, T. 152,2 ; Medini 1981b, n° 8; Medini 1986, 109-125; Vermaseren 1989, n° 133.

I. 4. 3. Bronze cast appliqué shaped as the front of Attis's head. The eyes are created with deep incisions, and the pupils are marked with indentations, while the mouth has a rough expression. The length of the hair touches the chin. The reverse hollow space has a regular hemispherical shape. (fig. 79)

Archaeological Museum in Zadar. Inv. No 391 (4701).

Dimensions: height 0.027 m, width 0.021 mm.

Date: second-third century A. D.

Literature: Medini 1968, 155-6, n° 12, T. IV; Medini 1977, 200-201; Medini 1978, 741, T. 152,3 ; Medini 1981b, n° 9; Medini 1986, 109-125; Vermaseren 1989, n° 134.

I. 4. 4. Bronze cast appliqué shaped as the front of Attis's head. The locks of hair are expressed as incisions and they reach the chin. The reverse side is a hemispherical hollow space. (fig. 80)

Archaeological Museum in Zadar. Inv. No 400.

Dimensions: Height 0.027 m, width 0.021 mm.

Date: second-third century A. D.

Literature: Medini 1968, 156, n° 13, T. IV; Medini 1977, 200-201; Medini 1978, 741, T. 152,4 ; Medini 1981b, n° 10; Medini 1986, 109-125; Vermaseren 1989, n° 135.

I. 4. 5. Bronze cast appliqué shaped as the front of Attis's head. The face is elongated with deeply incised eyes and mouth, while the nose is additionally flattened. The hair falls to the chin and is created by slanted incisions. (fig. 81)

Archaeological Museum in Zadar. Inv. No. 390 (4705).

Dimensions: height 0.027 m, width 0.020 mm.

Date: second-third century A. D.

Literature: Medini 1968, 156, n° 14, T. IV; Medini 1977, 200-201; Medini 1978, 741, T. 152,5 ; Medini 1981b, n° 11; Medini 1986, 109-125; Vermaseren 1989, n° 136.

I. 4. 6. Bronze cast appliqué shaped as the front of Attis's head. The top of the head is sharply processed. The locks of the hair go under the cap at the level of the temples, with locks on the back of the head reaching the chin. The reverse side is filled with remains of scorched materials, and the edges are damaged. (fig. 82)

Archaeological Museum in Zadar. Inv. No. 394 (4697).

Dimensions: height 0.036 m, width 0.030 mm.

Literature: Medini 1968, 156, n° 15, T. IV; Medini 1977, 200-201; Medini 1978, 741, T. 152,1 ; Medini 1981b, n° 12; Medini 1986, 109-125; Vermaseren 1989, n° 137.

1. 4. 7. Bronze cast appliqué shaped as the front of Attis's head. The cap is flattened at the front, so the cap point is missing. The facial details are accented with deep incisions; the nose is shaped as a triangle, while the forehead is tied with a band. Just as the previous appliqué, this one also has a poor quality of production. (fig. 83)

Archaeological Museum in Zadar. Inv. No. 396 (4691).

Dimensions: height 0.031 m, width 0.027 m.

Date: second-third century A. D.

Literature: Medini 1968, 155, n° 16, T. IV; Medini 1981b, n° 13; Medini 1986, 109-125; Vermaseren 1989, n° 138.

I. 4. 8 High-quality Bronze cast appliqué shaped as the front of Attis's head. The cap is decorated with irregularly spaced openings. The eyes are in deep hollows and the pupils are indented. There are also indentations on the upper lip as well. The reverse side is filled with lead. The object used for connection is visible. (fig. 84)

Archaeological Collection in Nin.

Dimensions: height 0.025 m. width 0.022 m.

Date: second-third century A. D.

Literature: Medini 1981b, n° 14; Medini 1986, 109-125; Vermaseren 1989, n° 139.

I. 4. 9. Stone plate with a relief made in white limestone. The upper edge and the right side are damaged, while the reverse side is roughly flattened. There are three vertical bands on the front left side, and they follow the left edge and the lower part of the body. At the right side there is a deep relief of a male figure in a sitting position with crossed legs. The upper part of the body and the head are missing. It was discovered in the foundation of the Medieval Church of St. Cross.

Dimensions: height 0.540 m, length 0.780 m, thickness 0.23 m

Date: first-second century A. D.

Literature: Medini 1989, 19-31.

I. 5. *IADER* (modern Zadar)

I. 5. 1. A fresco room used in the service of the Mother Goddess cult. It was discovered within the bounds of the Roman buildings on the Forum, 70 m south-west of the Capitol, among which there is a room with a mosaic floor and a cistern. The dimensions of the room are small - 5.20 m long, 3.45 m wide, while the preserved walls average 2 m. This room was at a somewhat lower level than the neighbouring room. The fresco painted on the walls of the room has a very high quality of artistic expression, and its style is similar to the third Pompeian style. Fourteen individuals were identified, although there is a plausibility that there were more, judging by the number of fragmented representations of limbs and other elements of the composition. Magna Mater is represented *en face* with her hair tied in a *crobylos*, wearing a dress with yellow-golden colour, with two lions beside her. Her figure is larger than the rest, and it stands out by the treatment of colours and the deep shadows. The preserved figures include one bearded individual with a strong expression, a male individual stepping on a snake with his right leg, a head of a younger man in a profile with a lifted left hand, *symplegma* of a man and a woman and a Corybant in an ecstatic dance, with a goat and a bull next to him. The fresco is framed with a floral bordure. (figs. 117-124)

Archaeological Museum in Zadar. Lost

Date: beginning of the second century A. D.

Literature: Suić 1965a, 353 – 355, Pl. 74, 75, 353-355, pl. 74, 1-5, pl. 75, 1-4; Suić 1965b, 100-104, fig. 8,9, 114-122, fig. 17, 18; Medini 1978, 742, pl. 153, 1-2; Medini 1981b, n° 15; Cambi 2002, 191, fig. 296, 297.

I. 5. 2. Fractured inscription in the fresco room. (fig. 22)

Magn[ae Deorum Matris]

Archaeological Museum in Zadar.

Dimensions: length 0.30 m, height 0.29 m, thickness 0.02 m.

Date: second century A. D.

Literature: Suić 1965a, 355, fig. 1; Suić 1965b, 100-102, fig. 7; Medini 1978, 742, pl. 153, 3; Medini 1981b, n° 16; Vermaseren 1989, n° 140.

I. 5. 3. Inscription from an unknown location in Zadar.

>   *D(is) M(anibus)*
>   *L(ucio) Barbunteio*
>   *Demetrio archig(allo)*
>   *Salonitano qui*
> 5   *annis XVII usq(ue) ad*
>   *ann(um) LXXV integr(e)*
>   *sacra confecit*
>   *Barbunteia Thallu*
> 10 *sa C[al]istera patrono*
>   *Pientiss(imo) posuit*

Lost.

Date: end of the second-beginning of the third century A. D.

Literature: CIL III 2920a; Graillot 1912, 235-6, n° 4, 492, n. 11; Suić 1965b, 100; Medini 1981b, n° 17; J. Medini 1981a, 15-28; Vermaseren 1989, n° 141.

I. 6. *ASSERIA* (modern Benkovci)

I. 6. 1. Limestone dedicational *ara* with an inscription. The upper left and the lower left parts are damaged. At the front there is a high relief of a man with a cape over the forearm. The face is destroyed, while the body is slightly turned to the right. The person holds a cornucopia in the left hand, and an ascia in the right. On the right hip there is a relief of a mug, with a ram's head and a knife to the right. (fig. 19)

>   *...[M(atri)] M(agnae)...*
>   *Q(uintus) Petronius*
>   *Philippus*

Archaeological Museum in Zadar.

Dimensions: height 0.620 m, width 0.410 m, thickness 0.300 m.

Date: second half of the second century.

Literature: CIL III, 9935; Graillot 1912, 491, Duthoy 1969, 13, 7; Medini 1978, 743f, pl. CLIV, 1; Schillinger 1979, 67, 57; Medini 1981b, n° 20; Vermaseren 1989, n° 145.

I. 7. *BLANDONA* (modern Biograd)

I. 7. 1. Bronze cast appliqué shaped as the front of Attis's head, discovered in a grave. The locks of the hair reach the chin. There is a hemispherical hollow space on the reverse side. (fig. 85)

Dimensions: height 0.035 m, width 0.029 mm.

Date: second - third century A. D.

Literature: Medini 1978, 743, T. 152, 6; Medini 1981b, n° 19; Medini 1986, 109-125; Vermaseren 1989, 146.

I. 8. *HADRA* (modern Medviđa)

I. 8. 1. Grey limestone head probably from Attis's sculpture, discovered in Medviđa. In the section between the cap and the forehead there are 40 pierced openings in two irregular rows, with several pierced openings between them. (fig. 90)

Private collection in Obrovac.

Dimensions; height 0.62 m, width 0.115 m, thickness 0.30 m.

Date: second half of the second century-beginning of the third century A. D.

Literature: Medini 1977, 195-205; Medini 1978, 747-750, tab. 156, 1-3; Medini 1981b, n° 22; Vermaseren 1989, n° 144.

I. 9. *BURNUM* (modern Kistanje)

I. 9. 1. Two fragments of a marble relief which probably were part of the Metroon at the western side of the earlier praetorium of the military camp. The frieze consists of at least three scenes separated with a band, while only the right end is preserved. Despite the damage, we can still recognize a composition of Cybele and Attis in the moment of his emasculation in the centre of the relief. The god is represented standing under a tree, naked holding his right hand between the legs. He has a Phrygian cap on the head. Cybele is facing him, dressed in a himation which she holds with the left hand, while her right hand is at the level of her head. She has a ring crown in the shape of city walls and a veil. On each of the sides of the frieze there are fields with the image of Attis in mourning. The only preserved detail in the right field is a part of the head with a recognizable Phrygian cap, while the left field contains the whole figure of Attis dressed in an oriental garment without attributes.

The fragments were first located in the Museum of Knin, now mostly lost, with only a small part located in the Archaeological Museum in Zadar. (fig. 93)

Dimensions: height 0.70 m, width 1.80 m, thickness 0.29 m.

Date: second half of the second century A. D.

Literature: Reisch 1913, 119-121, fig. 33; Schober 1923, 215; Medini 1978, 744-5, Pl. 155,1; Vermaseren 1966, 37; Vermaseren 1977a, 143; Medini 1981b, n°24; Vermaseren 1989, n°147.

I. 10. *TRAGURIUM* (modern Trogir)

I. 10. 1. Head of a stone sculpture, probably Attis.

Lost.

Dimensions: Unknown

Literature: AEMÖ IX 1885, 57; Graillot 1912, 493, n. 1; Medini 1981b, n° 26; Vermaseren 1989, n° 150.

I. 10. 2. White limestone fragment of Attis's sculpture in an oriental garment. (fig. 72)

City Museum in Trogir.

Dimensions: height 0.800 m.

Date: first-third century A. D.

Literature: BASD XXVII 1904, 22, pl. IV; Cambi 1980, n° 10, 11, 956; Medini 1981b, n° 27; Vermaseren 1989, n° 151.

I. 10. 3. White limestone inscription plate. (fig. 12)

    L(ucius) Stalli(us)
    Secundus (sex) [vir]
    Aug(ustalis) et Stallia Cal[lir(hoe)]
    Uxor cum liberis a[edem]
5   *Matri Magnae vo[to]*
    suscepto fecerunt [s(ua) p(ecunia)]

Archaeological Museum in Split. Inv. No. A 1371.

Dimensions: height 0.610 m, width 0.660 m, thickness 0.105 m.

Date: first-second century A. D.

Literature: BASD 11 (1888), 10, n° 5; CIL III 2676=9707; *BASD* 19 (1896), 88; Graillot 1912, 493, n. 1; Medini 1981b, n° 28.

I. 11. *SALONA* (modern Solin)

I. 11. 1. Fragment of a white limestone plate with an inscription field without profiled border. (fig. 8)

> ...*ius P(ublii) l(ibertus) Phileros*
> *[sex]vir*
> ...*l(iberos) [I]meros*
> *[sev]ir*
> 5 ... *deae barbaricae*
> *[f]ac(iendum) coer(averunt) idemq(ue)*
> ..*[dedicaverun]tq(ue).*

Archaeological Museum in Split. Inv. No. A 2866.

Dimensions: height 0.500 m, width 0.500 m, thickness 0.080 m.

Date: beginning of the first century A. D.

Literature: CIL III 14663,2; Graillot 1912, 493; Medini 1981b, n° 30; Šašel Kos 1999, 82.

I. 11. 2. White limestone plate with an inscription field and a simple relief border.

Discovered on the right bank of the Jadro River, close to the spring. (fig. 17)

> *Matri Magnae*
> *cognationis*
> *C(aius) Turranius Cronius*
> *sevir August(alis)*
> 5 *voto suscepto aedem et*
> *aram d(e) s(ua) p(ecunia) fecit et expolit*
> *idemque dedicavit.*

Archaeological Museum in Split. Inv. No. A 311.

Dimensions: height 0.570 m, width 0.750 m, thickness 0.065 m.

Date: first-second century A. D.

Literature: Frankfurter 1884, 111, 28; CIL III 8675; Kubitschek 1896, 88; Drexler in Rocher, *Myth.Lex.* II, col. 2922; Waltzing 1899, 98, 296; Graillot 1912, 492-3; Dessau 1916, 4105; Vermaseren 1977a, 143; Schillinger 1979, 63f; Medini 1981b, n° 31; Medini 1985, 7, n° 3; Vermaseren 1989, n° 165; Šašel Kos 1999, 83.

I. 11. 3. Marble inscription plate.

> *P(ublius) Iulius Rufus*
> *aedem Matr(is)*

> *Mag(nae) d(e) s(ua) p(ecunia) f(aciendam) c(uravit)*
> *idemq(ue) dedic(avit).*

Discovered in *Salona*, afterwards transported to Trogir. Lost.

Date: first-second century A. D.

Literature: CIL III 1953; Kubitschek 1896, 87; Drexler in Rocher, *Myth.Lex.* II, col. 2922; Graillot 1912, 492; Schillinger 1979, 62; Medini 1981b, n° 39; Vermaseren 1989, n° 157; Šašel Kos 1999. 83.

I. 11. 4. Marble inscription plate.

> *L(ucius) Statius L(uci) f(ilius)*
> *Facula quinq(uennalis)*
> *Matri Deum*
> *aedem d(e) p(ecunia) s(ua) f(ecit)*
> 5 *ex voto.*

Discovered in *Salona*, currently in the Archaeological Museum in Padua.

Date: first - second century A. D.

Literature: CIL III, 1954; Kubitschek 1896, 88; Graillot 1912, 492; Schillinger 1979, 62, 44; Medini 1981b, n° 32; Vermaseren1989, 156; Šašel Kos 1999, 83.

I. 11. 5. White limestone inscription plate.

> *Iunia Rhodine*
> *cum coniuge et fil(io/ filia?)*
> *D(eum) M(atri) M(agnae) aedem refecit*
> *et ampliavit v(oto) s(uscepto) s(olvit) -*
> *l(ibens) m(erito).*

Archaeological Museum in Split. Inv. No. A 2175.

Dimensions: height 0.340, width 0.580 m, thickness 0.120 m.

Date: first-second century A. D.

Literature: Kubitschek 1896, 41-42; CIL III 14243; Graillot 1912, 493; Schillinger 1979, 64, 48; Medini 1981b, n°, 33; Vermaseren 1989, n° 158; Šašel Kos 1999, 83.

I. 11. 6. Sacrificial altar with an inscription in a secondary use in a private residence in Klis. The original location of discovery is probably by the Jadro river.

> *Curia Pris-*
> *Ca Matri Magnae*
> *fanum rifecit*
> *signa posuit laro-*
> 5 *phorum cymbala*
> *tympana catillum*

forfices aram dat l(ibens) [a(nimo)].

Archaeological Museum in Split. Inv. No. A 866.

Date: first-second century A. D.

Literature: CIL III 1952=8567; Kubitschek 1896, 87; Drexler in Rocher, *Myth.Lex.* II, col. 2922; Graillot 1912, 492; Dessau 1916, 4106; Vermaseren 1977a, 142f; Schillinger 1979, 62, 42; Medini 1981b, n° 34; Vermaseren 1989, n° 166; Šašel Kos 1999. 83.

I. 11. 7. Grey limestone sacrificial altar with an inscription on the front. There is a shallow relief on the sides. On the left side, lined from the top to the bottom there are a dolphin, patera and a dog with the front paw pressed to a pillar, while on the right there are a fish, a bowl and once again a dog with a paw pressed to a pillar. Discovered in Klis.

> *Servilia M(arci) f(ilia)*
> *Copiesilla*
> *aediculam M(atris) Mag(nae)*
> *faciendam curavit*
> 5 *ipsa inpe(n)sa sua quam*
> *voverat pro ea M(arcus) Cot-*
> *inus Certus*
> *vir eius.*

Archaeological Museum in Split. Inv. No. A 2038.

Period: first-second century A. D.

Literature: CIL III, 13903; BASD 1985, 3; Kubitschek 1896, 87; Drexler in Rocher, *Myth.Lex.* II, col. 2922; Hepding 1903, 189; Dölger 1922, 442; Graillot 1912, 493; Dessau, 1916, 4106; Vermaseren 1977a, 143; Schillinger 1979, 63, 42; Medini 1981b, n° 40; Vermaseren 1989, n° 167; Šašel Kos 1999, 83.

I. 11. 8. Fragment of a white limestone sacrificial altar from *Salona*.

> *M(atri) [M(agnae)]*
> *C(aius) Agri[us...]*
> *et Agria...*
> *templu[m...]*
> 5 *vetusta[te corruptum]*
> *item Mat[ris imagines]*
> *duas cogna[tio...]*
> *p(ecunia) l. - easde[m...]*
> *sumptu su[o restituerunt].*

(According to J. Medini, 'Cognationes Salonitanae', *Godišnjak* 23, Centar za balkanološka ispitivanja 21 (1985), 7, n° 4 M. J. Vermaseren, CCCA VI, n° 151)

> *M(atri) [d(eum) M(agnae)]*
> *C. Agri[us -]*
> *et Agria[-]*

> *templu[m Matris Magnae -]*
> 5 *vetusta[te corruptum restituerunt]*
> *item Mat[ris statuas-]*
> *duas cogna[tas...]*
> *p(ondo) l(ibras) (duas) easde[m... arg(enteas)]*
> *sumptu su[o posuerunt-].*

(According to M. Šašel Kos, *Pre-Roman Divinities of the Eastern Alps and Adriatic,* Ljubljana 1999, 83.)

Archaeological Museum in Split. Inv. No. A 5510.

Dimensions: height 0.340 m, width 0.200 m, thickness 0.140 m.

Date: second century A. D.

Literature: Rendić Miočević 1953, 261; Medini 1981b, n° 35; Medini 1985, 7, n° 4; Vermaseren 1989, n° 155; Šašel Kos 1999, 83.

I. 11. 9. Fragment of an epistyle with partially preserved inscription field from *Salona*.

> *...[t]empl(um) M[atris Magnae]*
> *...ullinu[s]...*
> *vacat.*

Archeological Museum in Split. Inv. No. A 2476.

Dimensions: Height of the letters 0.110 m

Literature: CIL III, 14675; BASD 22 (1899) 9; Medini 1981b, n° 36; Vermaseren 1989, n° 154; Šašel Kos 1999, 84.

I. 11. 10. Fragment of a limestone inscription from *Salona*.

> *M(atri) I(deae) M(agnae)...*
> *nomine...*
> *.[sa]cerdos M.*

Archaeological Museum in Split. Inv. No. A 1190.

Dimensions: height 0.340 m, width 0.250 m, thickness 0.080 m.

Literature: CIL III, 8810; BASD 9 (1886), 146 n° 146; Graillot 1912, 493; Medini 1981b, n° 37; Vermaseren 1989, n° 159.

I. 11. 11. White limestone inscription plate framed in a regular relief bordure. Discovered in an antique well in a vicinity of the church of St Lovro, along with a statue of Cybele.

> *M(atri) M(agnae)*
> *cognatio*
> *fanum d(e) su(o) v(ota)*

ampliavit.

Archaeological museum in Split.

Dimensions: height 0.270 m, width 0.370 m, thickness 0.100 m.

Literature: Bulić 1923, 83-84; Zeiler 1929, 211; Schillinger 1979, 274, 688; Medini 1981b, n° 43; Medini 1985, 7-8, n° 5; Vermaseren 1989, n° 168; Šašel Kos 1999, 84.

I. 11. 12. White limestone sacrificial altar. (fig. 16)

> *V(iribus) V(alentibus) B(onis) s(acrum)*
> *M(arcus) Ulp(ius) At-*
> *talus*
> *collector*
> *cognatio*
> *nis ex p(ecunia) m(ultatitia)*
>
> *V(eneri) V(ictrici) B(onae) s(acrum)*

Archaeological Museum in Split. Inv. No. A 322.

Dimensions: height 0.890 m, width 0.290 m, thickness 0.260 m.

Date: second-third century A. D.

Literature: CIL III 8678; Graillot 1912, 282; Zeiller 1929, 210-11; Medini 1981b, 8-11; Medini 1985, 8, n° 6.

I. 11. 13. Fragment of a funerary sacrificial altar with an inscription.

> *D(is) M(anibus)*
> *...Aur(eilius) Maximianus Sa...*
> *...[col]legio dendrof[orum]*
> *...do ux[or]...*

Archaeological Museum in Split. Inv. No. A 389.

Date: second-third century A. D.

Literature: CIL III 8823; Waltzing 1899, 99, 302; Graillot 1912, 493; Марић 1933, 76; Schillinger 1979, 64, 48a; Medini 1981b, n° 41; Vermaseren 1989, n° 160.

I. 11. 14. Middle section of a white limestone funerary sacrificial altar. There is an inscription field framed in a profile at the front. The lower corners have a depiction of a kantharos sprouting vine tendrils with leaves and grapes. The tendrils are connected at the middle, above the inscription field, while under it there is an acanthus tendril with the leaves and rosettes. Each of the side fields have a figure of Attis, the left one being totally damaged, while on the right one we can see the pedum, part of the right leg and the top of the Phrygian cap. (fig. 107)

> *Q. Aeronio*
> *Firmino d(e)f(uncto)*
> *ann. XIIII mes. IIII*
> *Q. Aeronius Crescens*
> 5 *Caetrania Firma paren(tes)*
> *filio pientiss(imo) lib(ertis) lib(ertabus)q(ue) suis.*
> *Inuida Parcarum series liuorque malignus*
> *bis septena mea[e] ruperunt stamina lucis .*
> *Parcite iam lachrimis, miseri soliq(ue) parentes:*
> *sat fletus uestros prima fauilla bibit.*
> *Corpus habent cineres, animam sacer abstulit aer.*

Archaeological Museum of Split. Inv. No. A. 132.

Dimensions: height 0.838 m, width 0.735 m, thickness 0.520 m.

Date: second half of the second century A. D.

Literature: CIL III, 6384, Hepding 1903, 86, 25; Graillot 1912, 493; Lagrange 1919; 475; Medini 1981b, n° 58.

I. 11. 15. Middle section of a white limestone funerary sacrificial altar. The middle part has an inscription field framed with a profile. Under the inscription there is a decoration consisting of stylistically represented palm leaves, rosettes in the corners and big flowers in the middle. Each of the lower corners has a depiction of a kantharos sprouting vine tendrils with grapes and leaves decorating the rims. Each of the side fields, which are framed with a motif of vine tendrils, contains an antithetical relief of the figure of mourning Attis, and both of them are fairly damaged. Discovered along the previously described monument. (fig. 107, 108).

> *D(is) M(anibus)*
> *P(ublius) C(lodius) L(icinius)*
> *Et Aeliae f(eminae) c(arissimae) fecerun(t)*
> *se vivi poster(isque)*
> 5 *suis h(oc) m(onumentorum) h(eredes) -*
> *n(on) [s(equntum)]*

Archaeological Museum in Split. Inv. No. A. 134.

Dimensions: height 0.900 m, width 0.720 m, thickness 0.540 m.

Date: second half of the second century A. D.

Literature: CIL III 6390; Medini 1981b, n° 59.

I. 11. 16. White limestone architrave, part of the 'urbs orientalis Salonae'.

Discovered at the site Bakuša. (fig. 13)

[aedem Matri Magnae igne co]nsumptam res p(ublica) Salonitanorum
[ex voto sumptu suo a solo re]stituit.

Archaeological Museum in Split. Inv. No. A 2533.

Dimensions: length 2.800 m, height 0.600 m, width 0.520 m.

Date: second - third century A. D.

Literature: BASD XXI 1898, 141-144; CIL III 14674, Graillot 1912, 492; Medini 1981, n° 65; Vermaseren 1989, n° 153.

I. 11. 17. Lower part of white limestone statue of Cybele with an inscription on the base under the feet of the Goddess. The Goddess is sitting on a throne flanked by two lions. She is dressed in a chiton and himation ending with a tassel. The legs are parted. The upper part, most of the left-hand side and the heads and the bodies of the lions are missing, while the front corners of the base are damaged. (fig. 28)

    [C. Lu]tatius v(otum) l(ibens)
    [s(olvit) m(erito)]

Archaeological Museum in Split. Inv. No. B. 197.

Dimensions: height 0.250 m, width 0.280 m, thickness 0.190 m.

Date: second-third century A. D.

Literature: Medini 1981b, n° 44.

I. 11. 18 Lower part of a white limestone statue of Cybele. The Goddess is sitting on a throne with a high back-rest flanked with lions. She is dressed in a chiton and himation reaching her feet, which covers the front left-hand side of the chair. The left side of the lion's head is damaged. The Goddess has parted legs, holding a cylindrical object in her left hand, probably *cista mystica*. (fig. 29)

Archaeological Museum in Split. Inv. No. B. 101.

Dimensions: height 0.230 m, width 0.190 m.

Date: second-third century A. D.

Literature: *BASD* 20 (1897), 174-5; Medini 1981b, n° 45.

I. 11. 19. Lower part of a white limestone statue of Cybele. The Goddess is sitting on a low throne with parted legs and flanked with lions, which were not preserved except for the body of the left one. She is dressed in a chiton and a himation thrown over the left arm rest. In her left hand she is holding a cylindrical object, probably *cista mystica*. (fig. 30).

Archaeological Museum in Split. Inv. No. B. 125.

Dimensions: height 0.280 m, width 0.270 m.

Date: second-third century A. D.

Literature: Medini 1981b, n° 46.

I. 11. 20. White limestone statue of Cybele on a high base. The Goddess is sitting on a throne flanked with lions. The bodies of the lions are plastically represented and they are not leaning on the Goddess' legs. The Goddess is dressed in a chiton and a himation, while her legs are supported on a small square base. (fig. 31)

Archaeological Museum in Split. Inv. No. B. 212.

Dimensions: height 0.250 m, width 0.285 m.

Period: second-third century A. D.

Literature: *VAHD* 55 (1953); Medini 1981b, n° 47.

I. 11. 21. Lower part of limestone statue of Cybele.

The catalogue of J. Medini states that it is located in the Archaeological Museum in Split. Inv. No. B. 148. Probably lost.

Date: second-third century A. D.

Dimensions unknown.

Literature: Medini 1981b, n° 48.

I. 11. 22. Cybele statue.

The catalogue of J. Medini states that it is located in the Archaeological Museum in Split. Inv. No. B. 154. Probably lost.

Period: second-third century A. D.

Dimensions unknown.

Literature: Medini 1981b, n° 49.

I. 11. 23. White marble statue of Cybele discovered on the right bank of the Jadro river. The Goddess is sitting on a throne with a high back-rest which becomes narrower at the top, and lacks the arm-rests. There are lions sitting beside her, but only the back parts of their bodies were preserved. She is dressed in a high-girdled chiton and a himation over her knees. The head, the arms and the front part of the chest are missing. The right hand was additionally restored. (fig. 32, 33)

Archaeological Museum in Split. Inv. No. D. 372.

Date: second-third century A. D.

Literature: *BASD* 20 (1907), 99; Medini 1981b, n° 50.

I. 11. 25 White limestone statue of mourning Attis. The head and the lower parts of the legs are missing. The left hand is banded and pressed next to the body. The god is wearing a tunic and anaxyrides, with a cape over his shoulders. Revealed belly and genitalia. (fig. 70)

Archaeological Museum in Split.

Date: second - third century A. D.

Literature: Medini 1981b, n° 52; Cambi 2003, 513, fig. 3.

I. 11. 26. White limestone statue of Attis. The head and the lower parts of the legs are missing. The left hand is flexed and pressed to the body, while the right is banded in the elbow and touches Attis's head. The god is wearing a tunic and anaxyrides, with a cape over his shoulders. (fig. 71)

Archaeological Museum in Split. Inv. No. B. 168.

Dimensions: height 0.630 m.

Date: second-third century A. D.

Literature: Medini 1981b, n° 53.

I. 11. 27. Bronze Attis's statuette cast complete with the square base. Attis is leaning on a pillar, supporting on his right leg, while the left one is extended forward and to one side. He holds a syrinx in his right hand, and a pedum leaning on his shoulder in the left. The only garment he wears is the Phrygian cap. The eyes are marked by indentations. (fig. 99)

Archaeological Museum in Split. Inv. No. H. 379.

Dimensions: height 73 mm.

Date: second-third century A. D.

Literature: Jelić 1894, 167; Graillot 1912, 493; Medini 1981b, n° 54; Vermaseren 1989, n° 163; Žanić Protić 1988, 36, T. VI, 36; Cambi 2002, n° 168.

I. 11. 28. Bronze Attis statuette. Covered with a green patina on which is visible an impression of a cloth. Attis is standing on his right leg, while the left one is flexed and extended forward. He has a Phrygian cap on the head, and wears a tunic which is opened at the front revealing the belly. Attis has a tympanum on his back. (fig. 100)

Archaeological Museum in Split. Inv. No. H. 3413.

Date: first-third century A. D.

Literature: Medini 1981b, n° 55; Žanić Protić 1988, 37, T. VI, 37.

I. 11. 29. Bronze cast appliqué shaped as the front of Attis's head. The locks of hair reach the neck. The eyes are marked by indentations. The reverse side is filled with lead.

Archaeological Museum in Split. Inv. No. 767.

Dimensions: height 0.027 mm, width 0.021 mm.

Date: second-third century A. D.

Literature: Medini 1981b, n° 56; Medini 1986, 109-125.56; Vermaseren 1989, n° 164.

I. 11. 30. Bronze cast appliqué, much damaged. The assumption is that it is a representation of Attis's head.

Archaeological Museum in Split.

Dimensions: height 0.026 mm, width 0.021 mm.

Date: second-third century A. D.

Literature: Medini 1981b, n° 57; Medini 1986, 109-125; Vermaseren 1989, n° 164.

I. 11. 31 White limestone plate built into the old bell tower of the Cathedral in Split. The plate has a field bordered on the upper and lower side with a stair profile, and a field with a relief depiction of seven deities. The first on the right is the nude figure of Hercules with a lion skin in his right hand, next to him is Minerva dressed in a chiton, with a helmet on her head and a gorgonaeion on her chest. The Goddess supports herself with a long sceptre in her right hand, while in her left hand she holds a shield with an eagle on the front. In the middle there are representations of Jupiter and Juno, with an altar and an inscription between them, part of a figure and the wing-capped head of Mercury behind them. Jupiter has a toga over his hips and supports himself with a long sceptre in his right hand. Juno is dressed in a chiton and himation, holding a sceptre in the left hand, and she pours a sacrifice on the altar. To the right of Juno there is a figure of Mars in armour, leaning on a long spear, in front of him there is shield, while with his left suspended hand he holds a semi-circular shield. The last figure represents the deity (Cybele or *Tyche Salonitana*) with a 'mural' crown, dressed in a chiton with a himation over her. She holds a long sceptre in her right hand at the level of her head. (figs. 36, 37).

Mesc(enius)
Tert(ius)
felici(ter)

Archaeological Museum in Split. Inv. No. A. 2466.

Dimensions: length 0.340 m, width 0.750 m, thickness 0.300 m.

Date: second half of the second century A. D.

Literature: Lanza 1855, Pl. 2; Abramić 1950, 297-289; Cambi 1965, 57-8, Pl. XVIII-XIX; Medini 1981b, n° 63.

I. 11. 32 White marble sarcophagus with decorations on the front and the lateral surfaces. The front surface has a *tabula ansata* with an inscription and a floral ornament with a tendril. On each of the sides of the inscription there are representations of two Erotes, personifications of the seasons standing on high bases. The first figure on the left is Attis symbolizing Winter. He is depicted with wings, dressed in a short sleeved chiton, caped with a cloak with a button on the right shoulder, while on his head he is wearing a Phrygian cap. With his right hand he holds the hind legs of some kind of an animal, while in his right he holds a branch. Beside him there is the Erote of Spring, missing the head. The figure is winged and nude, except for the cloak thrown over the shoulders. He holds a flower in his right hand. There is a flower basket between these two figures. The other pair of Erotes as personifications of Summer and Autumn are to the right of the inscription plate. The first one is completely naked, holding a sickle in his right hand and a sheaf of hay in his left. The last of the Erotes has a cloak over the shoulders, and he pulls out a grape from a full basket. The lateral surfaces of the sarcophagus are decorated with identical nude and winged Erotes with garlands made of flower leaves and fruits which create the frames of the scenes. (fig. 113).

> *Homonea*
> *Zosime viva*
> *Sibi posuit et*
> *Septimio*
> 5 *Lucio marito suo*

Archaeological Museum in Split. Inv. No. D 20.

Dimensions: width 1.960 m, height 0.670 m, thickness 0.720 m.

Date: third century A. D.

Literature: Lanza 1856, 31, T. VIII, 2; Iveković 1910, T. 245; Gorenc 1952, T. 56, 57; Cambi 1960, n° 11; Cambi 2002, 166, fig. 254.

I. 11. 33. Two acroteria, parts of a white marble sarcophagus cover. There are representations of Erotes, personifications of the seasons. The first acroterium has the Erotes of Winter and Autumn, with an ascium in the lower right-hand corner. The Erot of Winter is winged Attis with crossed legs and a Phrygian cap on the head. He is dressed in a sleeveless chiton worn over a tunic with long sleeves and anaxyrides. He is holding a rod in the right hand, while leaning on a fruit basket with the left one. The Erot of Autumn is also with crossed legs and wears a cape. He embraces Attis with his right hand, and holds a large grape with the left. The other acroterium depicts the Erotes of Spring and Summer with their legs crossed. The first one is fully naked and stands on a low base, leaning on a flower basket with the left hand. The winged Erot of Summer has a cloak buttoned on the right side. He embraces the Erot next to him with the right hand, while in his left he holds a sickle turned upwards. (fig. 114)

Archaeological Museum in Split. Inv. No. D 483.

Dimensions: first acroterium - height 0.410 m, width 0.460 m

second acroterium - height 0.470 m, width 0.510 m.

Date: third century A. D.

Literature: Abramić 1929, 63; Cambi 1960, n° 12; Cambi 2002, 166-7, fig. 255, 256.

I. 11. 34. White limestone sarcophagus. On the middle of the front surface there is a *tabula ansata* without an inscription. To the left there is a representation of Attis wearing a Phrygian cap without the pulled forward top in the shallow niche. He is dressed in a girdled short tunic, with a cape over his shoulders. The legs are parted. Attis is leaning on a short overturned pedum, holding its end with the right hand, and his head with the left. There are three goats in front of him. To the right of the *tabula ansata* there is a representation of a male person with a short apron and an axe in his left hand, chopping something on a stump, while at the same time with his right hand he passes some object to the boy standing beside him. The upper right-hand corner has representations of an indistinguishable object of elongated shape. (fig. 111).

Archaeological Museum in Split.

Date: first half of the fourth century A. D.

Literature: Cambi 1970, 60-61, fig. 10-11; Medini 1981b, n° 60; Cambi 2003, 520, fig. 14.

I. 11. 35 Parapet temple with a hexagonal basis with a middle circular cell and pillars forming the exterior corridor west of the peristyle of Diocletian's Palace in Split. The diameter of the layout is 9.50 m. Part of the wreath with floral and animal motifs and a part of the coffered sealing of the external corridor were discovered. The temple also had a crypt. (fig. 14)

Literature: Marasović 1968, 18; Medini 1981b, n° 50a; Marasović 1994.

I. 11. 36. Fragment of a white marble lion's leg discovered in the crypt of the temple in the Diocletian's Palace in Split.

Institute for Protection of Cultural Monuments in Split.

Dimensions: length 0.360 m, width 0.130 m.

Literature: Medini 1981b, n° 50b.

I. 11. 37. Marble votive plate in relief of rectangular shape. The upper right corner is missing. It was discovered in 1897. The plate is framed with a simple border and divided into three zones. In the upper zone we have the following representations from left to right: a bird facing right, the bust of Sol, an eagle spreading its wings and positioned between two snakes and the bust of Luna. In the central, middle zone, there is a simple pillar on the left and the figure of Nemesis standing beside it and facing right. She is dressed in a long dress, with a veil on her head, while her right hand is in front of her mouth. A figure of a horseback rider turned to the right is represented beside her. He has a Phrygian cap on the head, and he wields a weapon – probably an axe – with his right hand. On his right there is the Goddess feeding a horse, while behind her there is a standing man holding an unidentified object. In the lower zone there are three images of large kraters going from left to right. There is a visible image of a piece of bread over the first one, while over the remaining two there are three lamps. Next in line is a tripod with a fish and a circular object which cannot be identified because part of the lower right corner of the monument is missing. (fig. 57).

Archaeological Museum in Split. Inv. No. D 215.

Dimensions: height 0.110 m, width 0.108 m, thickness 0.010 m.

Literature: Abramić 1940, 299, n° 1, pl. XIX, 1; Tudor 1960, 352, n° 166; Tudor 1969, 106, Pl. LIV.

I. 11. 38. Marble votive plate in relief with a rectangular shape and broken around the corners. In the upper part of the plate there is a bust of a deity, probably Sol or Luna, while at the right side there are two snakes facing an egg. The central figure under this zone is a horseback rider facing right. He is wearing a short tunic and a cape which flies in the wind. With his right hand he attacks a man lying under the hooves of the horse. Behind the rider we can see a male figure also wearing a short tunic and holding the tail of the horse. The Goddess is standing in front of the rider and she holds the bridles of the horse, while to her right there is an additional male head. (fig. 58).

Archaeological Museum in Split. Inv. No. D 73.

Dimensions: height 0.098 m, width 0.096 m, thickness 0.017 m.

Literature: Abramić 1940, 300, n° 2, pl. XIX, 2; Tudor 1960, 353, n° 167; Tudor 1969, 107, Pl. LIV.

I. 11. 39. Fragment of the right hand corner of a marble votive plate in relief. There is a recognizable kantharos flanked with snakes, which was probably the central image of the upper zone, while on its left there is a bust of a deity, probably Luna or Sol, facing right. We can notice three heads in the central zone – a woman, a bearded male, and a young man with a Phrygian cap. (fig. 59).

Archaeological Museum in Split.

Dimensions: height 0.070 m, width 0.083 m, thickness 0.016 m.

Literature: Abramić 1940, 300, n° 3, pl. XX, 3; Tudor 1960, 354, n° 168; Tudor 1969, 108, Pl. LV.

I. 11. 40. Fragment of the upper left-hand corner of a marble votive plate in relief. In the upper zone we notice a bust of a deity, while in the lower zone we can see only the heads and shoulders of two individuals. (fig. 60)

Archaeological Museum in Split.

Dimensions: height 0.077 m, width 0.053 m, thickness 0.016 m.

Literature: Abramić 1940, 300, n° 4, pl. XX, 2; Tudor 1960, 354, n° 169; Tudor 1969, 109, Pl. LV.

I. 11. 41. Fragment of the upper right part of a stone votive plate in relief. In the upper part there is a kantharos and the lower part of a bust of a deity, probably Sol or Luna. In the central zone going from left to right we can see two horse riders with a Phrygian cap and lifted left hand wielding a weapon, female head with a hand in front of the mouth (Nemesis) and the upper part of a male head with a Phrygian cap. (fig. 61)

Archaeological Museum in Split.

Dimensions: height 0.080 m, width 0.086m, thickness 0.023 m.
Literature: Abramić 1940, 300, n° 5, pl. XX, 5; Tudor 1960, 354, n° 170; Tudor 1969, 110, Pl. LVI.

I. 11. 42. Fragment of the lower left corner of a marble votive plate in relief. We can see a representation of a decapitated ram hanging from the tree, with the blood dripping in a kantharos. On the right there is a man skinning the ram. Behind him there is the ram's head and a rhomboid shape with horizontal lines. (fig. 62)

Archaeological Museum in Split.

Dimensions: height 0.067 m, width 0.082 m, thickness 0.015 m.

Literature: Abramić 1940, 301, n° 6, pl. XX, 4; Tudor 1960, 354, n° 171; Tudor 1969, 111, Pl. LVI.

I. 11. 43. Fragment of the upper semi-circular part of a marble votive plate in relief. The image is divided into two zones. In the central part of the upper zone there is a bird with two snakes beside her. On her left and on her right there are the busts of Sol and Luna. In the lower zone the central figure is the Magna Mater. She is approached by horseback riders from two sides. Behind the left one there is a female figure (Nemesis), while we can see two figures behind the right one – a man with a Phrygian cap and a woman. (fig. 63).

Archaeological Museum in Split.

Dimensions: height 0.053 m, width 0.097 m, thickness 0.020 m.

Literature: Abramić 1940, 302, n° 7, pl. XX, 1; Tudor 1960, 355, n° 172; Tudor 1969, 112, Pl. LVI.

I. 12. *TILURIUM* (modern Trilj)

I. 12. 1. White limestone stele. The architrave with the frieze and the gable are missing. The upper field framed with two pillars with a relief representation of a horseback rider galloping to the right in the upper part, while in the lower part there was an inscription, which is completely ruined. In the lower field there is a relief motif *porta inferi* formed out of four panels – in the upper part there are lion heads with door-knocker rings, while in the lower part an antithetical representation of Attis in a typical mourning posture. Discovered in a secondary use as a door of the mortuary of the local graveyard in Gardun. (fig. 68)

Archaeological Collection of the Franciscan Monastery in Sinj.

Dimensions: height 2.00 m, width 0.630 m, thickness 0.250 m.

Date: first century A. D.

Literature: Medini 1981b, n° 75; Medini 1984a, n° 3.

I. 12. 2. Fragment of a grey limestone stele. The gable and a part of the upper field are missing. The upper field is framed with two pillars and divided in two parts. The upper part had the torso of a departed man in deep relief, but only one part of the chests and the right hand are preserved, while in the lower section there is an inscription field with a profile. In the lower field there is a relief motif *porta inferi* formed out of four panels; in the upper part there are lion heads with door-knocker rings, while in the lower part an antithetical representation of Attis in a typical mourning posture. (fig. 67)

C(aius) Longinus C(ai) f(ilius)
Cor(nelia) Amblada
mil(es) leg(ionis) VII an(norum) LX
stip(endiorum) XXI h(ic) s(itus) e(st)
frater fratri

Archaeological Museum in Split. Inv No. A 1982.

Dimensions: height 1.730 m, width 0.860 m, thickness 0.265 m.

Date: first half of the first century, no later then 42 A. D.

Literature: CIL III, 9737; Hofman 1905, 57-58, n° 45, fig. 37; Medini 1981b, n° 76; Medini 1984a, n° 1; Sanader 2003, 509, Abb. 4; Tončinić 2004, n° 34.

I. 12. 3. Grey limestone stele. The inscription is in the upper field which is framed with pillars. Above it there is an architrave lying on stylistically represented Corinthian capitals, and above it there is a frieze with alternating motifs of weapons with the following order: *ocrea, scutum, pelta, scutum, galea, lorica, scutum, ocrea*. In the lower field there is a relief motif *porta inferi* formed out of four panels; in the upper part there are lion heads with door-knocker rings, while in the lower part an antithetical representation of Attis in a typical mourning posture.

Cn(aeus) Domitius Cn(aei) f(ilius)
Pessinunte an(norum) XLIV stip(endiorum)
XXV veteran(us)…en…iussit.

Built in a graveyard chapel in Gardun.

Date: middle of the first century A. D.

Literature: CIL III. 2710=9726; Hofman 1905, n° 43; Medini 1981b, n° 77; Medini 1984a, n° 2; Tončinić 2004, n° 12.

I. 12. 4. Inscription plate. Provenance unknown.

M(agnae) M(atri)
M(arcus) Cal(purnius) Pri(mus)
Et Treb(onia) Chr(este)
rest[ituerunt]

Archaeological Museum in Split. Inv. No. A 2052.

Date: second-third century A. D.

Literature: *BASD* 18 (1895), 18; CIL III 13927; Graillot 1912, 491; Medini 1981b, n° 78.

I. 13. SINJ

I. 13. 1. White limestone stele with an inscription. Its composition is divided into two parts. The upper is a triangle and a deep profile of a gable with a frieze. In the middle there is a high relief of Attis's head wearing a Phrygian cap. The acroteria were shaped like lions, but only the front claws are preserved. The frieze has a string of alternating kraters and two dolphins connected by their tails. There are two masks hanging on a string in the place where the tails are touching. In the middle field there is a medallion with a high profile of a figure of a young departed man with a ball in the right hand. The corners of this field have rosettes, while the medallion is also framed with ovum and astragals. The lower part contains two inscription fields, where only the upper one is framed with a simple classical relief border. (fig. 110).

> *C(ius) Laberius f(ilius)*
> *V[al]es ann(orum) VII*
> *h(ic) s(itus) e(st)*
>
> *Hunc titulum posuit tibi fidus amicus ultuma –*
> *quae potui debita persolvi*
> *Non dolere mater faciundum fuit properavit*
> *Aetas voluit hoc astrum meum vale et priores*
> *Atetate te tollant hunc luctum tibi*

Secondary use, facade of a private house in the Oslobođenje St. No. 16 in Sinj.

Dimensions: height 1.130 m, width 0.460 m, the height of the letters of the first inscription ranges from 0.039 m to 0.028 m, the height of the letters of the second inscription field is around 0.015 m.

Date: beginning of the second century A. D.

Literature: CIL III 2722=9729; Medini 1981b, n° 74; Medini 1984a, n° 4.

I. 14. *EPETIUM* (modern Stobreč)

I. 14. 1. White limestone statue of Cybele. The Goddess is sitting on a throne with a high back-rest. The legs are parted while the right one is slightly extended. She is dressed in a chiton and a himation which is thrown over the Goddess' legs. There were lions beside her legs, but they are almost totally missing.

Archaeological Museum in Split.

Dimensions: height 0.340 m, width 0.220 m

Date: second - third century A. D.

Literature: Medini 1981b, n° 68.

I. 15. VRLIKA

I. 15. 1. Inscription plate of undetermined shape and dimensions. Discovered in the church of St Peter.

> *Mat(tis) D(eum) [ae]d[em]*
> *Vitalis et Maximus frater*

Date: second-third century A. D.

Literature: CIL III 2755; Medini 1981b, n° 79.

I. 16. SRINJINE

I. 16. 1. Fragment of a white limestone inscription plate. The inscription field framed with a groove, while the last letters of the first three lines go over its edge.

> *...Lupula Statili[a]*
> *[tem]plum Matri Magn[ae] (sic)*
> *[deo]rum de su ore*
> *[stitui]t*
> 5 *cun suis fel(iciter) (sic)*

Archaeological Museum in Split. Inv. No. A 1860.

Dimensions: height 0.260 m, width 0.330 m, thickness 0.330 m.

Date: second-third century A. D.

Literature: *BASD* 11 (1888), 177, n° 105; CIL III 8544 = 12814; *BASD* 16 (1893), 33, n° 13; Medini 1981b, n° 67.

I. 17. PRIDRAGA

I. 17. 1. Fragment of a white limestone relief. The aedicule on the front side is preserved only with the left cannelured pillar with a small head on the right side. In the space of the aedicule there is a representation of a bearded deity with a Phrygian cap in a relief. He is wearing a long sleeved tunic, while the belly and the genitalia are revealed. He holds a snake flexed as the letter S in his left hand, while in the right a syrinx. The legs of the deity resemble goat legs. To the right of the deity there is a stag in a vertical posture. (fig. 92)

Museum of Old Croatian Monuments in Split

Dimensions: height 0.195 m, width 0.225 m, thickness 0.120 m.
Date: third century A. D.

Literature: Cambi 1968, 131-141; Medini 1978, pl. 154, 2; Medini 1981b, n° 21a; Selem 2005, 426-427.

I. 18. LEPURI

I. 18. 1. Fragment of a thicker limestone plate discovered in a secondary use. It was a part of a larger composition. The front side depicts mourning Attis in a typical posture holding the head with the right hand and leaning on the left. He wears a Phrygian cap on the head, a short tunic with long sleeves, a cape and anaxyrides. The cape is buttoned with a fibula on the right shoulder. Under the upper edge of the monument, to the right of Attis' figure, there is a decoration resembling one half of a stylistic leaf. The right lateral side is damaged. On the reverse there is a circular surface with two fish and five circular loaves of bread between the fish, and they are held by a hand which is preserved below the elbow. Above the upper fish, there are 4 objects of elongated shape resembling short sticks.

Archaeological Collection of the Franciscan Monastery in Sinj.

Dimensions: height 1.020 m, width 0.800 m, thickness 0.280 m.

Date: second - third century A. D.

Literature: Medini 1981b, n° 21.

I. 19. *ANDETRIUM* (modern Muć)

I. 19. 1. Bronze statuette of Attis. Attis is wearing a tunic buttoned with a large button, anaxyrides on the legs, and a Phrygian cap on the head. The belly and the genitalia are revealed. Attis is kneeling on the right knee and he is depicted at the moment after the emasculation. He has his left hand lifted high, and it is assumed that he holds the object for emasculating in it. (fig. 101)

Archeological Museum in Split. Inv. No. H 4975.

Dimension: height 85 mm.

Date: second-third century A. D.

Literature: Popović, Mano Zisi, Veličković and Jeličić 1963, 100, n° 129; Vermaseren 1977a, 142, fig. 78; Medini 1981b, n° 73; Vermaseren 1989, n° 149; Žanić Protić 1988, 35, T. VI, 35.

I. 20. 1. Bronze cast appliqué shaped as the front of Attis's head. The locks of the hair are parted at the forehead and they reach the chin. The face is oval, the eyes marked with indentations, the nose additionally flattened, the mouth slightly open.

Archaeological Collection in the Franciscan Monastery in Sinj.

Dimension: height 0.032 m, width 0.027 m.

Date: second-third century A. D.

Literature: Medini 1984a, n° 5; Medini 1986, 109-125.

I. 20. 2. Marble votive plate of rectangular shape and a rounded upper part discovered in 1882. The artistic image is divided into three zones. In the corners of the upper zone there are the busts of Luna and Sol, while in the middle there is a krater with two snakes drinking from it. The central figure in the second zone is the Great Goddess dressed in a chiton and himation, with quarter moons to the right and to the left of her head. She is holding the bridles of the horses which are on her left and right. The horses have riders dressed in tunics and capes flying in the wind. Under the hooves of the horses there are men supporting on the hands with the head facing down. Behind each of the riders we can see a human figure. There is a star between the heads of the riders and the figures. In the lower zone going from left to right there is a rooster, three circular objects, two stags, a tripod with a fish and three lamps, and an additional tripod with a stag's head. (fig. 64).

Archaeological Collection in the Franciscan Monastery in Sinj.

Dimension: height 0.092 m, width 0.160 m, thickness 0.013 m.

Literature: ÖJh XVII 1914, 148, fig. 135; Will 1955, 315, fig. 63; Tudor 1969, 113, Pl. LVII.

I. 21. BRAČ

I. 21. 1. Limestone plate with an inscription framed with a regular profile. Discovered in 1983 at the new cemetery in Škrip. (fig. 15).

> *M. M.*
> *MESCENIA P. F.*
> *TERTULLA PORTIC*
> *F. D. S. P.*

Brač Museum in Škrip.

Literature: Gjurašin 1989, 17; Gjurašin 1990, 252.

II. HISTRIA:

II. 1. *POLA* (modern Pula)

II. 1. 1. Limestone inscription plate in six parts, the lower right corner is missing. Elongated rectangular shape with a double profiled frame. Discovered in Pula, near the temple of Augustus. (fig. 18)

Dendrophoris
Polensium
C(aius) Laecanius
Theodorus
sacer[d]os M(atris) D(eorum) M(agnae) I(daeae)
lo[cu]m cum
sepultura dedit
in fr(onte) p(edes) XLII
in ag(ro) p(edes) LX[II?]

Lapidarium of the Archaeological Museum of Istra in Pula.

Dimensions: height 1.250 m, width 0.84 m, thickness 0.170 m.

Date: first century A. D.

Literature: Kandler 1855, 251; CIL V, 481; Weisshäupl 1901, 202, n° 90; Sticotti 1914, 290, n. 3; Gnirs 1915, 75, n° 105; Dessau 1916, 4172; Swoboda 1969, 205, n° 16; Degrassi 1970, 625; Vermaseren 1978, n° 247; Girardi Jurkić 1999 II, 3.8.1.

II. 1. 2. Funerary rectangular limestone stele with an aedicule with the face of the departed. On the right there is a relief figure of mourning Attis. On the left there is an additional figure which cannot be identified. On the lateral sides of the stele there are two ithyphallic herms with high caps in relief. There is an inscription under the aedicule. (fig. 73)

Obellia(e) Maximae

Lapidarium of the Archaeological Museum of Istra in Pula. Inv. No. A 313.

Dimensions: height 0.920 m, width 0.790 m, thickness 0.360 m.

Date: first century A. D.

Literature: Carli 1794, 193; Kandler 1855, 262; Reichel 1893, 4, n° 84; Weisshäupl 1901, 202; Gnirs 1912, 270; Sticotti 1914, 213; Degrassi 1970, 625; Vermaseren 1978, n° 248; Girardi Jurkić 1999 II, 3. 9. 5.

II. 1. 3. Funerary limestone *cippus*. At the front of the monument there is a relief image of Attis in a shallow rectangular aedicule. The deity has the characteristic mourning posture, the right hand located at the height of the waist, the left one holding the head, the legs crossed. He is wearing a tunic and a cape, with a Phrygian cap on the head. The aedicule is framed with a representation of the temple with an architrave and a gable, which is decorated with a rosette flanked with birds in the centre. The acroteria are shaped as palmettes. The lateral pilasters on both of the sides of the aedicule are decorated with a relief of a pine with a pinecone on the top, while the trunk is wrapped with snakes. The pilasters end in capitals with palmettes. At the lateral side of the monument there is a relief of a kantharos, sprouting vine branches and birds.

Lapidarium of the Archaeological Museum of Istra in Pula. Inv. No. A 261.

Dimensions: height 1.270 m, length 0.590 m, width 0.590 m.

Date: first - second century A. D.

Literature: Reichel 1893, 93, 94; Gnirs 1915, 91, n° 326, 327; Swoboda 1969, 204, n° 17; Vermaseren 1978, n° 246; Girardi Jurkić 1999 II, 3. 9. 6.

II. 1. 4. Funerary limestone *cippus*, almost identical with the previous. At the front of the monument there is a relief image of Attis in a shallow rectangular aedicule. The deity has the characteristic mourning posture, the right hand located at the height of the waist, the left one holding the head, the legs crossed. He is wearing a tunic and a cape, with a Phrygian cap on the head. The aedicule is framed with a representation of the temple with an architrave and a gable, which is decorated with a rosette flanked with birds in the middle. The acroteria are shaped as palmettes. The lateral pilasters on both of the sides of the aedicule are decorated with a relief of a pine with a pinecone on the top, while the trunk is wrapped with snakes. The pilasters end in capitals with palmettes. At the lateral side of the monument there is a relief of a kantharos, sprouting vine branches and birds.

Lapidarium of the Archaeological Museum of Istra in Pula. Inv. No. A 253.

Dimensions: height 1.190 m, length 0.590 m, width 0.591 m. (fig. 74)

Date: first-second century A. D.

Literature: Reichel 1893, 93, 94; Gnirs 1915, 91, n° 326, 327; Swoboda 1969, 204, n° 17; Vermaseren 1978, n° 246; Girardi Jurkić 1999 II, 3. 9. 7.

II. 1. 5. Limestone statue of Attis. The head and the legs are missing. The end of the right hand is damaged. The forearm suggests that it was flexed and slanted at the elbow, and it was probably supporting the head. Attis is dressed a chiton, worn over a longer shirt and girdled.

There is a cape over the shoulders, buttoned at the chest. The posture of the statue corresponds to the type Attis in mourning. (fig. 69).

Lapidarium of the Archaeological Museum of Istra in Pula. Inv. No. A 261.

Dimensions: height 1.115 m, width 0.520 m, thickness 0.310 m.

Date: second century A. D.

Literature: Jurkić 1978, T. I; Girardi Jurkić 1999, 3.9.1.

II. 1. 6. Limestone head of Attis. The face is bordered with long locks of hair which fall over the shoulders, with a Phrygian cap on the head. The eyes are circular without marks for the pupils. Bedazzled look and half open mouth. (fig. 65).

Exhibition of the Roman stone statuary in the temple of Augustus in Pula. Inv. No. A 4570.

Dimensions; height 0.330 m, width 0.210 m, thickness 0.235 m.

Date: second-third century A. D.

Literature: Swoboda 1969, 203f, n° 13, fig. 4; Vermaseren 1978, n° 245; Girardi Jurkić 1999, 3.9.2.

II. 2. *NESACTIUM* (modern Nezakcij)

II. 2. 1. Marble statue of Magnae Matris. The head, the right hand up to the middle of the upper arm, and the left forearm are missing. The Goddess is sitting on a throne, the legs are separated from the knees, while the left one is slightly flexed backwards and rests on the floor with the toes. She is dressed in a luxurious chiton and himation with a cape thrown over the right shoulder and the hips with one of its ends, and she is wearing sandals on her feet. There are traces of buttons on the shoulders. The throne is beautifully crafted with rounded connections, while the arm supports end in lion protomes. A flexed snake goes up the legs of the Goddess. The reverse is not worked. (fig. 5, 6)

Antique Collection of the Archaeological Museum of Istra in Pula, hall 2. Inv. No. A 5748

Dimensions: height 0.300 m, width 0.300 m, thickness 0.550 m

Date: first-second century A. D.

Literature: Mlakar 1978, 56; Girardi Jurkić 1999, 3.8.3.

II. 2. 2. Bronze statuette of Attis discovered in a residential building with an atrium. The deity is missing the head, while the surface is covered with green patina. This statue was identified as Attis according to the posture of the body and the Phrygian clothes.

Lost. The Inv. No. of the Antique Collection of the Archaeological Museum of Istra was not registered.

Dimensions: unknown.

Date: first-second century A. D.

Literature: Sticotti 1934, 332; Vermaseren 1978, n° 251; Girardi Jurkiæ 1999, 3.9.4.

II. 3. JESENOVIK

II. 3. 1. Part of a limestone dedicational *ara* with an inscription. The upper and lower edges are destroyed, while the left and the right side are partially detached. (fig. 7)

M(atri) Mag(nae)
deorum
[C(ai) V]alerii Optati
f(ilia) Felicula
[v(otum)] s(olvit) l(ibens) m(erito)

Lapidarium of the Archaeological Museum of Istra in Pula, hall 1. Inv. No. A 19.

Dimensions: height 0.420 m, width 0.150 m, thickness 0.190 m.

Date: second century A. D.

Literature: Degrassi 1933, 381; Degrassi 1936, 198; Swoboda 1969, 207, n° 19; Degrassi 1970, 625; Vermaseren 1978, n° 250; Girardi – Jurkić 1999, 3.8.2.

II. 4. Istra unknown

II. 4. 1. Limestone head of Attis. The lower part of the face is damaged. There is a Phrygian cap on the head with traces of hair showing under the rim. The eyes are half shut without marks for the pupils. The place of discovery is unknown. (fig. 66)

Archaeological Museum of Istra in Pula. Inv. No. A 4824.

Dimensions: height 0.190 m, width 0.155 m, length 0.131 m.

Date: second-third century A. D.

Literature: Girardi Jurkić 1999, 3.9.3.

III. PANNONIA:

III. 1. *SISCIA* (modern Sisak)

III. 1. 1. Bronze bust of Attis. The oval face of the deity is framed with locks of hair, the pupils are marked with deep holes which were probably filled with silver. He wears a Phrygian cap on the head, decorated with spiral motifs and a six-pointed star. (fig. 102)

Archaeological Museum in Zagreb. Inv. No. 53

Dimensions: height 0.200 m

Date: second century A. D.

Literature: Brunšmid 1914, n° 53; Popović, Mano Zisi, Veličković and Jeličić 1963, 99, n° 126; Selem 1980, n° 17, t. XVIII; Vermaseren 1989, n° 121; Tóth 1989, n° 11; Cambi 2002, 115.

III. 1. 2. Bronze statuette of Attis, probably used as an appliqué. The feet and the upper part of the pedum, which he holds with the left hand, are missing. The right leg is extended forward, while he holds the mask of Cybele in his raised right hand. The hair is in locks, while he wears a Phrygian cap on the head. Attis is dressed in a tunic which is opened at the front, and anaxyrides. Visible castration. (fig. 94)

Archaeological Museum in Zagreb. Inv. No. B 54.

Dimensions: height 0.090 m.

Date: second century A. D.

Literature: Brunšmid 1914, n° 54; Selem 1980, n° 11, t. XXXVI; Selem 1981, 187–194, fig. 2; Vermaseren 1989, n° 118; Tóth 1989, n° 13.

III. 1. 3. Bronze statuette of Attis, probably used as an appliqué. Attis is holding the mask of Cybele above his head with both his hands. The hair is styled in locks; a Phrygian cap is on the head. He is wearing a tunic opened at the front, and anaxyrides. Visible castration. (fig. 95)

Archaeological Museum in Zagreb. Inv. No. B 55.

Dimensions: height 0.10 m

Date: second-third century A. D.

Literature: Brunšmid 1914, n° 55; Selem 1980, n° 12, t. XXXVI; Selem 1981, 187–194, fig. 3; Vermaseren 1989, n° 119; Tóth 1989, n° 14.

III. 1. 4. Bronze statuette of Attis. Attis is leaning with his back on a pillar. He wears a Phrygian cap on the head, a tunic with a fibula revealing the belly and genitalia, and anaxyrides on the legs. The right hand is raised and the head rests on it; the figure holds a pedum in his extended left hand. (fig. 98)

Archaeological Museum in Zagreb. Inv. No. B 56.

Dimensions: height 0.056 m.

Date: second century A. D.

Literature: Brunšmid 1914, n° 56; Selem 1980, n° 13, t. XXXVI; Selem 1981, 187–194, fig. 3; Vermaseren 1989, n° 120; Tóth 1989, n° 15.

III. 1. 5. Tombstone with inscription

> *Aurel(iae) Veneriae ob hon(orom)*
> *et florem iuventu(tis) subit(a)*
> *morte occupatae mi pient(issimae)*
> *virgini P(ublius) Ael(ius) Iulianu(s)*
> 5 *ex num(ero) colleg(ii) dendro(phorum)*
> *v(ivus) f(ecit)*

Lost

Dimensions: unknown

Date: second half of the second century - first half of the third century A. D.

Literature: CIL III 10853; Kukuljević, 1873, 142; Graillot 1912, 487; Selem 1980, 201f, n° 8; Tóth 1989, n°10.

III. 1. 6. Marble tomb stele with an inscription. The lower part is missing. The shallow triangle gable has the image of Medusa with snakes wrapped around the neck and one acanthus leaf on each of her sides. Along the lateral walls of the gable there are remains of lion figures, each of them holding a ram's head in the claws. Under the gable there is an aedicule framed with half pillars with Corinthian capitals. The niche contains relief representations of five torsos, two male, one female, and two girls, with the inscription field under them. The lateral sides of the monument are decorated with wavy vine with leaves and grapes. (fig. 46, 47)

> *Domu (!) (a)etern(a)e et perpe-*
> *[t] u(a)e securitati. C(a)enius*
> *...ianus, v(ir) e(gregius), v(ivus) f(ecit) Fl(avio) Tibe-*
> *[rian]i[co?] q(ui) v(ixit) an(nos) XXX,*
> 5 *...ni(a)e Urs(a)e, q(uae) v(ixit) an(nos) IIII,*
> *...q(uae) v(ixit) an(nos)*

Dimensions: height ranging from 0.960 m to 1.345 m, width 0.875 m, thickness ranging from 0.190 m to 0.22 m.

Date: third century A. D.

Literature: Katančić 1826, 440; CIL III, 3985; Gregl and Migotti 2000, 119 – 164.

III. 1. 7. Bronze cast appliqué shaped as the front of Attis head. (fig. 87)

Archaeological collection of Mateja Pavletič.

Date: second-third century A. D.

Literature: Balen, Demo, Ožanić, Radman – Livaja, Rendić – Miočević and Uranić 2003, n° 161.

III. 1. 8. Fragment of a limestone statue of Attis. Preserved head with the Phrygian cap and the right shoulder of the statue with a fibula. The right chin bears traces of the hand which is broken off.

Archaeological Museum in Zagreb. Inv. No. 16.

Dimensions: height 0.350 m.

Literature: *VAHD* 7 (1906-1907), 222, 16, Selem 1980, 202f, 10; Tóth 1989, n° 12.

III. 1. 9. Lead votive plate with an oval shape. Discovered in 1896 in the river Kupa. A small part of the upper left corner is missing. The scene is divided in three zones and bordered with a double edge – the outer one is with a fishbone motif, while the inner one consists of circles. In the centre of the upper zone is the figure of Nemesis with the right hand in front of her mouth, and wearing chiton and himation. The bust of Sol with a seven-rayed crown is on her left, while on her right there is the bust of Luna with a quarter-moon on her head. To the left of Sol there is a tripod with three circular objects and a stag's head, while to the right of Luna there is a rooster. The central position of the central zone is for the Great Goddess on a pediment, dressed in a long chiton and holding a cloth over her loins. On each of her sides there is a rider dressed in a tunic and a cape flying in the wind, with a Phrygian cap on the head. They salute the Goddess with the right hands. Under the hooves of each of the horses there are figures of man in a laid position. Behind the left rider there is a figure of a rooster, while behind the right one a figure of a man with raised hand. The third zone depicts a cribolium – a man skinning a ram hanging from the tree. On the right there is a lion, while on the left there is a candelabrum with a lamp, a kantharos and one indistinguishable object. (fig. 53)

Archaeological Museum in Zagreb.

Dimensions: diameter 0.075 m.

Literature: AE XXIII 1903, 335, n° 60; VAHD VIII 1905, 124; Iskra – Janošić 1966, IV, 8; Tudor 1969, 162, Pl. LXXIV.

III. 1. 10. Lead votive plate in relief, with a rectangular shape identical to the one from Dalj. See III. 8. 1.

Archaeological Museum in Zagreb.

Dimensions: height 0.094 m, width 0.076 m, thickness 0.002m.

Literature: AEMÖ III 1879, 171, n° 7; AE XXIII 1903, 348, n° 49; VAHD VIII 1905, 121, fig. 3; Iskra – Janošić 1966, I, 11; Tudor 1969, 163.

III. 1. 11. Lead votive plate in relief with a rectangular shape. The scene consists of four zones and it is bordered with pillars with Corinthian capitals supporting an arch filled with a frieze consisting of oval decoration. The upper zone depicts Sol flanked with stars and standing in a quadriga, dressed in a tunic and fluttering cape, while he has a crown with seven rays on the head. He salutes the world with the right hand, while he holds a globe and a whip in the left. The central figure of the middle zone is the figure of Great Goddess dressed in a chiton and himation. On her left and on her right there are riders dressed in tunics and fluttering capes. They salute the Goddess with their right arms. The rider on the left has a Phrygian cap on the head. Behind the rider on the right there is a female figure, probably Nemesis, holding her hand in front of the mouth, while behind the rider on the right there is an armed warrior. Under the hooves of the right horse there is a figure of a man lying on his back, while under the hooves of the left horse there is a large fish. In the third zone there are three men sitting around a table with a cloth and a fish located in front of the Goddess. To the right there are naked men holding their hands, while on the left there is a tree with a decapitated ram hanging from the branches. There is a male figure skinning the ram, while behind him there is a person with a ram mask. In the last zone we can see a tripod with a fish, krater flanked with a lion and a snake, and a rooster going from left to right.

Vienna Museum.

Dimensions: height 0.095 m, width 0.080 m, thickness 0.003 m.

Literature: Tudor 1969, 164

III. 1. 12. Marble votive plate with an oval shape in relief. Discovered in the Sava river in 1875. The scene is divided into two zones. The central image of the upper zone is the Great Goddess standing behind a table with a fish. On her left and on her right there are figures of bearded riders in tunics and with Phrygian caps on the heads. Under the hooves of each of the horses there is a man lying on his back. In the lower zone there are blurred images of a rooster, a standing woman (Nemesis?), a chair and an animal, probably lion. (fig. 54)

National Museum in Budapest.

Dimensions: height 0.090 m, width 0.074 m, thickness 0.007 m.

Literature: AE XXIII 1903, 336, 33; Tudor 1969, 160, Pl. LXXIII.

III. 1. 13. Fragment of a marble votive plate of oval shape discovered in 1913. The only remaining fragment of the central scene is the tripod with a fish, and the lower body of the rider and the horse, with a man lying on his back under the hooves and with the hands and knees lifted. In the field underneath we can see two men facing each other with their hands connected horizontally. There is yet another male head on the background between them. There is a representation of a galloping horse on the right, and there is a lamp above. (fig. 55)

Archeological Museum in Zagreb.

Dimensions: height 0.102 m, width 0.080, thickness 0.007 m.

Literature: VHAD XVI 1935, 65, n° 14; Tudor 1969, 161, pl. LXXIII

III. 2. *MURSA* (modern Osijek)

III. 2. 1. Marble statue of Cybele. The Goddess is sitting on a throne with her legs supported on the lion lying in front of her. She is dressed in a chiton and a himation thrown over her loins. The head and the arms of the Goddess, as well as the head of the lion, are missing. High-quality production, probably an import. (fig. 39)

Museum of Slavonia in Osijek. Inv. No. 7923.

Dimensions: height 0.820 m, width 0.420 m, thickness 0.340 m.

Date: first half of the second century A. D.

Literature: Pinterović 1967b, 67-79, tab. 1.; Selem 1980 207f, 15, pl. XXXVII; Vermaseren 1989, n° 124; Tóth 1989, n° 111.

III. 2. 2. Terracotta statue of the Goddess on a throne with a high back-rest. Dressed in a long dress with a waist girdle, and a veil on her head reaching the knees. No other attributes which could identify Cybele.

Museum of Slavonia in Osijek. Inv. No. 2606.
Dimensions: height 0.210 m, width 0.115 m, thickness 0.400 m.

Literature: Pinterović 1967b, 72; Selem 1980 209, 17, pl. XXXVIII; Vermaseren 1989, n° 125; Tóth 1989, n° 112.

III. 2. 3. Fragment of the crown of the funerary monument with two lions. The left part with one of the lions and a female head is preserved. There is a ram's head visible under the claws of the lion. The only preserved part of the lion on the right is the hind leg. (fig. 40).

Museum of Slavonia in Osijek. Inv. No. 7316.

Dimensions: height 0.560 m, length 0.630 m, width 0.240 m.

Date: second - third century A. D.

Literature: Pinterović 1967b, 73; Selem 1980, 208, 16; Tóth 1989, n° 118; Kulenović and Muštra 2002, T. I, 3.

III. 2. 4. Lead votive plate in relief, a rectangular shape identical to the one in Dalj. See bellow III. 8. 1.

Museum of Slavonia in Osijek

Dimensions: height 0.094 m, width 0.076 m, thickness 0.002 m.

Literature: AE 1905, 12, n° 73; Tudor 1969, n° 145.

III. 3. POPOVAC

III. 3. 1. Crown of a funerary monument of a pair of lions. Both lions are fully preserved, while they hold rams' heads under their claws. In the middle there is a female head with kalathos. (fig. 41)

Private collection in Popovac.

Date: second-third century A. D.

Literature: Pinterović 1967b, 73; Tóth 1989, n° 26; Kulenović and Muštra 2002, T. I, 4.

III. 4. GORNJI BUKOVEC

III. 4. 1. Fragment of the crown of a funerary marble stele with a pair of lions. (fig. 43).

Private collection in Gornji Bukovec

Dimensions: height 0.450 m, length 0.780 m.

Date: second-third century A. D.

Literature: Gregl 1996, n° 5.

III. 5. GABAJEVA GREDA (KOPRIVNICA)

III. 5. 1. Crown of a funerary monument with a pair of lions. The monument is unfinished. Under the claws of the lions there are ram's heads. In the middle there is a female head with kalathos. (fig. 42)

Dimensions: length 1.600 m, width 0.680 m, height 0.440 m.

Date: second-third century A. D.

Literature: Kulenović and Muštra 2002, 143-152, T. I, 1.

III. 6. ODRA

III. 6. 1. Marble funerary stele with an inscription, divided into three parts. The triangle gable contains the head of the Medusa with snakes wrapped around the neck and figures of eagles on both of sides. The two lateral acroteria have a shape of a lion holding a ram's head, while the middle acroterium is missing. Under the gable there is the architrave beam with a relief frieze with floral motif, framed with a simple profile. In the middle of it there is a rectangular inscription field, bordered with half pillars on profiled bases ending in Corinthian capitals. In the lower part there is a relief of three figures – a mounted rider in a warrior's armament with a spear in the right hand and flanked with two antithetical Erotes in a mourning posture, leaning on turned torches and with their legs crossed. (fig. 44)

> T. FL.ATERIGIS
> FIL.ATEBODVO
> AN.LXXV.VE//R
> EMERITO.COH.I/.VA/
> EQ.CORNVGLARIO
> PRAEF.ET.CRISPI/
> CONIVG.AN.L/
> ET.FL.AVGVURINO.NEP
> AN V
> H . F. C

Dimensions: height 1.870 m, width 0.855 m, thickness 0.165 m.

Date: end of the first century A. D.

Literature: Rendić – Miočević 1993, 28-31; Gregl and Migotti 2000, 130-1, fig. 8

III. 7. DONJI ČEHI

III. 7. 1. Limestone funerary stele with an inscription. In the upper part there is a triangle gable with the figure of Medusa in the middle. The acroteria are shaped as lions with rams' heads under their claws. The upper part is almost completely obliterated. In the middle zone there is an aedicule with portraits of four deceased: three adults and one child. There is an inscription under the decorative frieze. (fig. 45)

Lapidarium of the Archaeological Museum in Zagreb.

> D(is) M(anibus)
> Valens, et
> Melania
> Caeserni. Aviti
> servi. sibi. et
> Valentinae. an(orum). XX
> et. Donico. an(norum) II
> filiis. Rarissimi(s)

Dimensions: height 1.86 m, width 0.810 m, thickness 0.220 m.

Date: middle of the second century A. D.

Literature: Gregl 1996, n° 1; Gregl and Migotti 2000, Fig. 7.

III. 8. *TEUTOBURGIUM* (modern Dalj)

III. 8. 1. Lead votive plate in relief with a rectangular shape. It was discovered in 1932. The complex scene is framed with Corinthian pillars supporting the arch filled with a frieze with oval-shaped decorations. The upper corners outside the framed field have two coiled snakes. The central figure is the Great Goddess dressed in a chiton and himation, she is holding a cloth band in her hands, with the ends loosely falling on both sides, while she wears large earrings. On the left and on the right there are riders facing the Goddess, and saluting her with the left hand. They are dressed in tunics and both of them have capes flying on the wind. The rider on the left has a Phrygian cap on the head. There is a large fish under the hooves of the rider on the right, while under the hooves of the other rider there is a man lying on his back. The central scene is flanked with human figures in a long dress with the right hand in front of her mouth (probably Nemesis), while on the right there is a figure of a warrior with armour, sword, helmet and a shield. Above this central composition there is a field ending in a semi-circular arch with the representation of Sol in a quadriga, larger than the rest of the figures. He is wearing a tunic and a cape flying in the wind, with a seven-rayed crown on his head. He salutes the world with the right hand, while holding a globe and a whip in the left. The head of the deity is flanked with large eight-pointed stars. Under the central scene there is a field with a central representation of three men sitting on a bench around a table covered with draped tablecloth. There is a fish on the table. On the right side there are two young men approaching the table holding their hands, while on the left there is a tree with a decapitated ram hanging from it. One man is skinning the ram, while the one standing next to him has a ram mask on the head. In the lower zone going from left to right there are images of a fish, a kantharos flanked with a lion and a snake and a rooster. (fig. 51).

Archaeological Museum in Zagreb

Dimensions: height 0.094 m, width 0.076 m, thickness 0.002 m.

Literature: VHAD XVI 1935, 64, fig. 4; Wenzel 1961, 91; Iskra-Janošić 1966, 19, tab. II, fig. 1; Tudor 1969, n° 132. Pl. LXIII.

III. 9. *CIBALAE* (modern Vinkovci)

III. 9. 1. Lead votive plate in relief, with a shape of an aedicule, fractured in two parts. The upper part is shaped as a gable with acroteria at the two corners. The gable has an image of a fish flanked with stars. There is also one star in the two acroteria. The main scene is underneath, in the rectangular framed field. The upper zone has an amphora, while to the left and to the right of it there are snakes. On the outmost left side there is a bust of Luna with a quarter-moon on the shoulders, while on the right we can see Sol with a crown with rays. In the middle of the main zone there is a figure of the Great Goddess standing on a base with spread out arms and dressed in two-piece dress. On the two sides there are horse riders dressed in tunics, with fluttering capes and Phrygian caps on their heads. Under the hooves of both of the horses there is a man lying on his back. Behind the rider on the right there is a figure of Nemesis down to her waist, while behind the left one there is a figure of a warrior. In the middle of the lower zone there is a scene of cribolium – a man skinning a ram hanging from the tree. On the left there is a knife stuck in the ground, a candelabrum with a lamp, and a tripod with two cups and a round object, probably bread. On the right there is a kantharos, three round objects, and a rooster above the ram's head. (fig. 52).

Archaeological Museum in Zagreb.

Dimensions: height 0.088 m, width 0.074 m, thickness 0.004 m.

Literature: AEMÖ III 1879, 23, n° 2, AEMÖ 127, n° 8; VHAD VI 1902, 149, fig. 76; AE XXIII 1903, 353, 58; Iskra-Janošić 1966, III 2, tab. IV, fig. 1; Tudor 1969, n° 137, Pl. LXV.

III. 10. *CARNACUM*

III. 10. 1. Lead votive plate in relief discovered in 1819, identical to the one in Dalj. See III. 8. 1.

National Museum in Budapest.

Dimensions: height 0.094 m, width 0.076 m, thickness 0.002 m

Literature: AE XXIII 1903, 347, 47; Iskra-Janošić 1966, I, 8; Tudor 1969, n° 141.

III. 11. GRAČANICA

III. 11. 1. White marble votive plate in relief. The upper part has a circular shape. The scene is divided into two zones. The central figure of the upper zone is the Great Goddess with lifted hands, while to the left and to the right of her there are riders dressed in tunics and fluttering capes, with Phrygian caps on their heads. Under the hooves there are human figures lying on their backs. In the lower zone under the Goddess there is a tripod with an unknown object, a kantharos and several other objects and animals which cannot be identified because of the damaged relief. (fig. 56).

Tourist Office in Nova Gradiška.

Date: third century A. D.

Dimensions: height 0.180 m, width 0.170 m, thickness 0.035 m.

Literature: Pinterović 1975, 131-133, fig.1.

Figure 1. Figure of a Goddess *kourotrophos* from *Nesactium* (After Kovač 1992, fig. 28).

Figure 2. Terracotta figure of the Goddess from Çatal Hüyük (After Vermaseren 1977a, p. 5).

Figure 3. Double head from *Nesactium*, 6th – 5th centuries B.C. (After Kovač 1992, fig. 16).

Figure 4. 'The twins' from Çatal Hüyük (After Mellaart 1963, pl. XX, d).

Figure 5, 6. Marble statue of Magnae Matris (After Girardi Jurkić 1972, tab. VII, fig. 1, 2).

Figure 7. Altar with inscription from Jesenovik (After Girardi Jurkić 1999, tab. XXXII, 3.8.2).

Figure 8. White limestone plate with an inscription field from *Salona* (Photo courtesy of the Archaeological Museum in Split).

Figure 9. White marble *epistylium* with an inscription in a frame from *Senia* (After Degmedžić 1952, fig. 1).

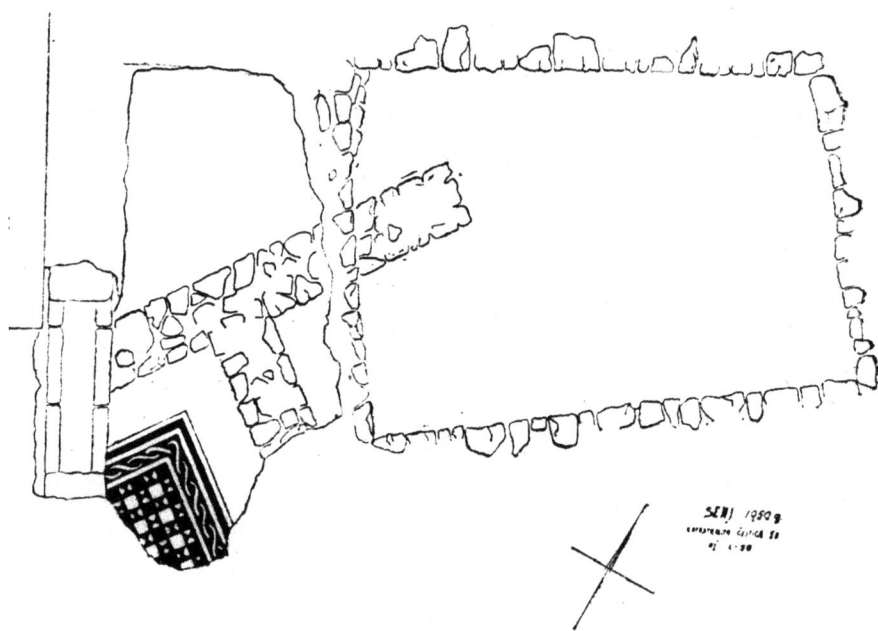

Figure 10. Layout of the Metroon wools and the house with mosaic floor from *Senia* (After Degmedžić 1952, fig. 5).

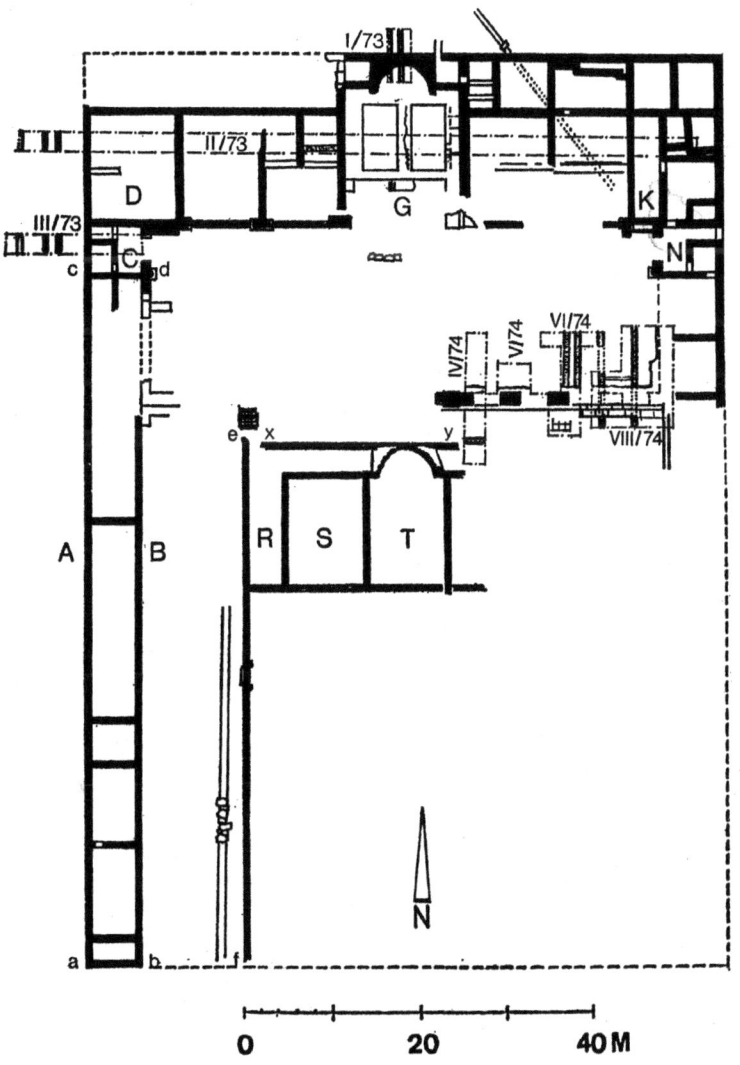

Figure 11. Layout of the *Burnum* Forum (After Medini 1989a, 263).

Figure 12. White limestone inscription plate from Trogir (Photo courtesy of the Archaeological Museum in Split).

Figure 13. White limestone architrave, part of the 'urbs orientalis Salona'
(Photo courtesy of the Archaeological Museum in Split).

Figure 14. Remains of the temple in the Diocletian's palace (After Marasović 1994, 112).

Figure 15. Limestone plate with an inscription from Brač (After Gjurašin 1989, 17).

Figure 16. White limestone sacrificial altar from *Salona*
(After Medini 1985, tab. II).

Figure 17. White limestone plate with an inscription from *Salona*
(After Medini 1985, tab. I, fig. 2).

Figure 18. Limestone inscription plate from Pula
(After Girardi Jurkić 1999, tab. XXXII, 3.8.1).

Figure 19. Limestone dedicational *ara* with an inscription and a relief from *Asseria*
(After Medini 1993, tab. XII, 1).

Figure 20. Square pool from the Zadar Forum (After Suić 1965b, fig. 16).

Figure 21. Reconstruction of the balustrade of the Capitolium in Zadar (After Suić 1965b, fig. 14).

Figure 22. Inscription from Zadar (After Medini 1993, tab. XI, fig. 3).

Figures 23 and 24. Marble statue of Cybele from *Senia* A (left) and *Senia* B (right) (After Cambi 2002, 140).

Figures 25 and 26. Marble head from *Senia* (After Cambi 1993, fig. 1, 2).

Figure 27. Head of the Goddess from Samothrace (After Welch 1996, pl. 89, a).

Figure 28. Lower part of white limestone statue of Cybele with an inscription from *Salona* (Courtesy of the Archaeological Museum in Split).

Figure 29. Lower part of a white limestone statue of Cybele from *Salona* (Courtesy of the Archaeological Museum in Split).

Figure 30. Lower part of a white limestone statue of Cybele from *Salona* (Courtesy of the Archaeological Museum in Split).

Figure 31. White limestone statue of Cybele from *Salona* (Courtesy of the Archaeological Museum in Split).

Figures 32 and 33. White marble statue of Cybele from *Salona* (Courtesy of the Archaeological Museum in Split).

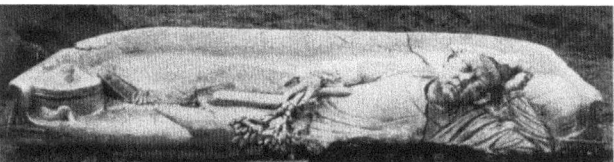

Figure 34. Lid of the sarcophagus of the *archigallus* from Ostia (After Vermaseren 1977a, p. 66)

Figure 35. Relief from Lanuvium (After Vermaseren 1977c, 466, pl. CCXCVI).

Figure 36. Marble slab on the old bell-tower from the Cathedral in Split (After Abramić 1950, fig. 3).

Figure 37. Detail of the relief from the
Cathedral in Split (After Abramić 1950, fig. 4).

Figure 38. Statue from the National museum in
Bucurest (After Vermaseren 1977b, 37, pl. XXV).

Figure 39. Marble statue of Cybele from Osijek (After Pinterović 1967b, fig. 1).

Figure 40. Fragment of the upper part of a stele from Osijek (After Kulenović and Muštra 2002, tab. 1, 3).

Figure 41. Upper part of the stele from Popovac (After Kulenović and Muštra 2002, tab. 1, 4).

Figure 42. Upper part of the stele from Gabajeva greda (After Kulenović and Muštra 2002, tab. 1, 1).

Figure 43. Drawing of the upper part of the stele from Gornji Bukovec (After Gregl 1996, n. 5).

Figure 44. Funerary monument from Odra
(After Gregl and Migotti 2000, fig. 8).

Figure 45. Funerary monument from Donji Čehi
(After Gregl and Migotti 2000, fig. 7).

Figure 46. Funerary monument from *Siscia* (After Gregl and Migotti 2000, fig. 3b).

Figure 47. Upper part of a funerary monument from *Siscia* (After Gregl and Migotti 2000, fig. 4).

Figure 48. Tombstone of Lucius Egnatuleus Florentin (After Gregl and Migotti 2000, fig. 9).

Figure 49. Figure of a horse rider from *Nesactium* (After Kovač 1992, fig. 25).

Figure 50. Hellenistic clay plaque from Samothrace (After Lawall 2003, fig. 4. 10).

Figure 51. Lead votive plate from Dalj (After Iskra-Janošić 1966, 19, tab. II, fig. 1).

Figure 52. Lead votive plate from Vinkovci
(After Iskra-Janošić 1966, 19, tab. IV, fig. 1).

Figure 53. Lead votive plate from Sisak
(After Tudor 1969, 162, pl. LXXIV).

Figures 54 and 55. Marble votive plates from Sisak (After Tudor 1969, 160, 161, pl. LXXIII).

Figure 56. Marble votive plate from Gračanica (After Pinterović 1975, fig. 1).

Figures 57-63. Marble votive plates from *Salona*
(After Tudor 1969, 106, 107, pl. LIV; 108, 109, pl. LV; 110, 111, 112, pl. LVI).

Figure 64. Marble votive plate from Čitluk (After Tudor 1969, 113, pl. LVII).

Figure 65. Limestone head of Attis from Pula (After Girardi Jurkić 1999, tab. XXXIV, 3.9.2).

Figure 66. Limestone head of Attis from unknown provenance, *Histria* (After Girardi Jurkić 1999, tab. XXXIV, 3.9.3).

Figure 67. Grey limestone stele from *Tilurium* (After Cambi 2003, fig. 1).

Figure 68. White limestone stele from *Tilurium* (After Cambi 2003, fig. 2).

Figure 69. Limestone statue of Attis from Pula (After Girardi Jurkić 1978, tab. 1).

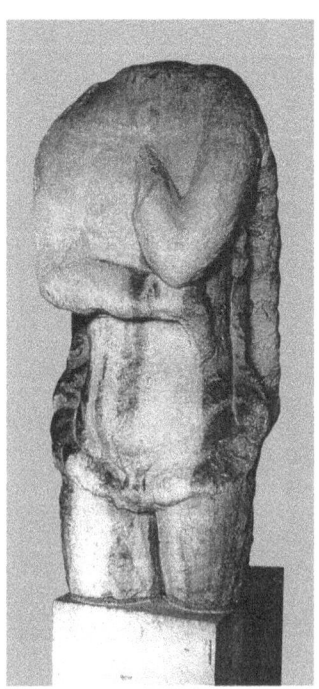

Figure 70. White limestone statue of mourning Attis from *Salona* (After Cambi 2003, fig. 3).

Figure 71. White limestone statue of Attis from *Salona* (Photo courtesy of the Archaeological Museum in Split).

Figure 72. White limestone fragment of Attis' sculpture from *Traugurium* (After Vermaseren 1989, 151, pl. XXXIV).

Figure 73. Funerary monument of Obellia Maxima from Pula (After Girardi Jurkić 1999, tab. XXXIV, 3.9.5).

Figure 74. Funerary limestone cippus from Pula (After Girardi Jurkić 1999, tab. XXXV, 3.9.7a).

Figure 75. Terracotta pinecones from the Palatine (After Vermaseren 1977c, 74, 75, pl. LIII).

Figure 76. Terracotta *glans penis* from Palatine (After Vermaseren 1977c, 69, 70, 71, pl. LII).

Figure 77. Handle of a bronze patera from north of France (After Vermaseren 1986, 467, pl. CLVII).

Figures 78-84. Bronze cast appliqués from *Aenona* (After Medini 1968, tab. IV, 11-16).

Figure 85. Bronze cast appliqué from *Blandona* (After Medini 1993, tab, X, 2).

Figure 86. Bronze cast appliqué from the archaeological collection Benko Horvat (After Koščević 2000, 197).

Figure 87. Bronze cast appliqué from Sisak (After Balen *et al* 2003, 161).

Figure 88. Bronze cast appliqué from Louvre (After Vermaseren 1977b, 118, pl. LXXX).

Figure 89. Bronze cast appliqué from Russi, Gallia Cispadana (After Vermaseren 1978, 214, pl. LXXXVI).

Figure 90. Stone head from *Hadra* (After Medini 1977, tab. I).

Figure 91. Marble head of Mithras from Ostia (After Vermaseren 1977c, 396, pl. CCXLVI).

Figure 92. Relief slab from Pridraga, drawing (After Cambi 1968, fig. 2).

Figure 93. Relief from *Burnum* (After Medini 1993, tab. XIII, 1).

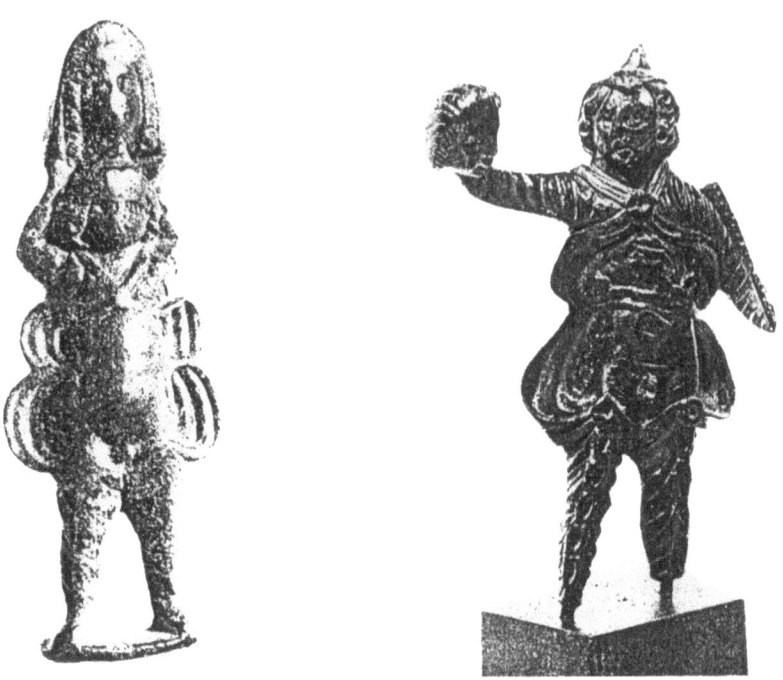

Figures 94 and 95. Bronze figurines of Attis from Sisak (After Selem 1981, figures, 1, 2).

Figure 96. Bronze figure of Attis from Louvre (After Vermaseren 1966, pl. XXXIX).

Figure 97. Bronze figure of Attis from Berlin (After Vermaseren 1966, pl. XL).

Figure 98. Bronze figure of Attis from Sisak (After Selem 1981, fig. 3).

Figure 99. Bronze figure of Attis from *Salona* (After Cambi 2002, 168).

Figure 100. Bronze figure of Attis from *Salona* (Photo courtesy of the Archaeological Museum in Split).

Figure 101. Bronze figure of Attis from *Andetrium* (After Vermaseren 1977a, p. 78).

Figure 102. Bronze bust of Attis from Sisak (After Cambi 2002, 164).

Figure 103. Small bust of a god from Sisak (Photo D. Doračić 2005).

Figure 104. Terracotta figure of Attis from Tarsus (After Vermaseren 1987, 815, pl. CLXXV).

Figure 105. Terracotta figure of Attis from Tarsus (After Vermaseren 1987, 836, pl. CLXXX).

Figure 106. Marble antefix from Nemausus (After Vermaseren 1986, 328, pl. CXV).

Figure 107. Tombstone of Aeronius Firmin from *Salona* (After Cambi 2003, fig. 3).

Figures 108 and 109. Tombstone from *Salona* (Photo courtesy of the Archaeological Museum in Split).

Figure 110. Funeral monument from *Tilurium* (After Cambi 2003, fig. 5).

Figure 111. Fragment of a late antique sarcophagus from *Salona* (After Cambi 2003, fig. 14).

Figure 112. Terracotta figurine from Myrina (After Vermaseren 1987, 498, fig. 29).

Figure 113. Sarcophagus from *Salona* with a depiction of Attis winter (After Cambi 2002, 254).

Figure 114. Acroterium of a sarcophagus from *Salona* with a depiction of Attis winter (After Cambi 2002, 256).

Figure 115. Detail from the 'Dumbarton Oaks sarcophagus' (After Vermaseren 1977c, 315, pl. CLXXXII).

Figure 116. Sarcophagus from Emporium (After Vermaseren 1986, 210, pl. LXIV).

Figure 117. Fragment of the fresco from Zadar with the image of the Goddess (After Suić 1965b, fig. 8, 9).

Figures 118 - 123. Fragments of the fresco from Zadar (After Suić 1965a, pl. 74, 3; pl. 75, 1, 3, 4).

Figure 124. Fragment of the fresco from Zadar a depiction of a Corybant (After Suić 1965a, pl. 75, 2).

Figure 125. Sculpture from Boğazköy (After Naumann 1983, Taf. 7, 1).

Figure 126. Terracotta figurine from Egina, (After Vermaseren 1982, 527, fig. 18).

Figures 127, 128. Terracotta lamps from south Italy (After Vermaseren 1978, 138, pl. XLIII; 144; pl. XLVI).

Figure 129. Relief from Piraeus (After Vermaseren 1982, 270, pl. LXIII).

Figure 130. Funeral slab from Luna (After Vermaseren 1978, 204, pl. LXXVII).

Figure 131. Relief from Thracia dedicated to Bendis (After Маразов 1994, 21).

Figure 132. Hellenistic relief from Lebadeia (After Naumann 1983, Taf. 28, 1).

Figure 133. Golden diadem from Neapolis (After Vermaseren 1987, 896, pl. CXCVIII).

Figure 134. Upper part of a monument from Tasos (After Vermaseren 1977a, p. 28).

Figure 135. Roman plaque from Egypt (After Naumann 1983, Taf. 31, 1).

Figure 136. Silver lanx from Parabiago (After Musso 1983, Tav. 4).

Figure 137. Marble plate from Gaul (After Burkert 1987a, fig. 9).

Figure 138. Terracotta figurine from Tegeia (After Vermaseren 1982, 488, pl. CXLV).

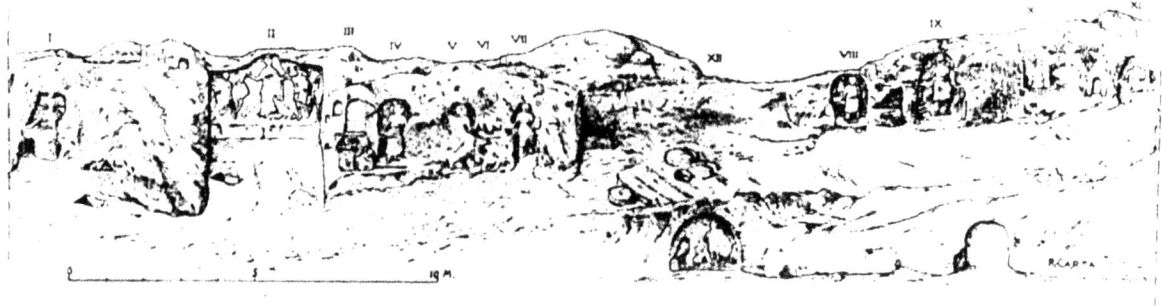

Figure 139. Rock reliefs from Colle Orbo (After Sfameni Gasparro 1996, fig. 2).

Figure 140. Relief from Colle Orbo (After Vermaseren 1978, 153, pl. LIII).

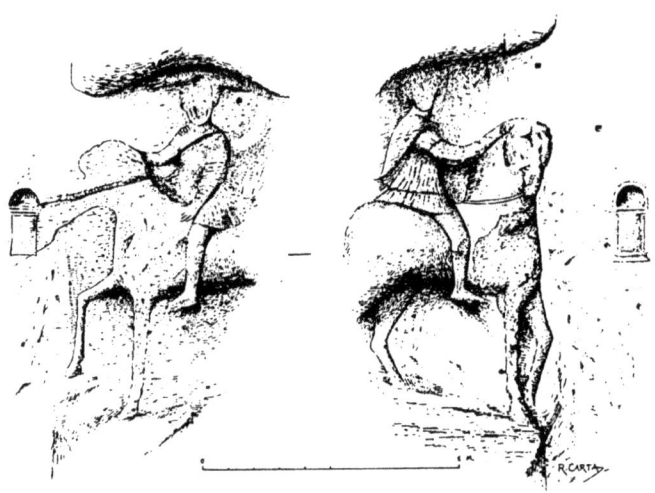

Figure 141. Relief from Colle Orbo (After Vermaseren 1978, 154, pl. LIII).

Figure 142. Relief from Cyzicus (After Vermaseren 1977b, 69, pl. LI).

Figure 143. *Ara Pietatis Augustae*, detail (After Vermaseren 1977, p. 32).

Figure 144. Statue of a Corybant from Ostia (After Vermaseren 1977c, 377, pl. CCXXXV).

ABREVIATIONS

AASH	Acta Antiqua Academiae Scientorum.
AC	L'Antiquté Classique.
AE	Archeologiai Ertesitö.
AEMÖ	Archäologisch – epigraphische Mittheilungen aus Österreich-Ungarn, I-XX (1870-1898), Wien.
AMSI	Atti e memorie della Società istriana di archeologia e storia Patria, Parenzo – Venezia – Trieste.
ANRW	Aufstieg und Niedergang der Römischen Welt.
AOF	Archiv für Orientforschung. Internationale Zeitschrift für die Wissenschaft vom Vordern Orient.
Arh. vest.	Arheološki vestnik.
AS	Anatolian Studies. Journal of the British Institute of Archaelogy at Ankara.
AZ	Archäologische Zeitung.
BASD	Bulletino di Archeologia e Storia Dalmata.
BJ	Bonner Jahrbücher des Rheinischen Landesmuseums in Bonn und des Vereins von Altertumsfreunden im Rheinlande.
CCCA	Corpus Cultus Cybelae Attidisque.
CIL	Corpus Inscriptionum Latinarum.
CMRDM	Corpus Monumentorum Religionis Dei Menis.
CMRED	Corpus Monumentorum Religionis Equitum Danuvinorum.
CPh	Classical Philology.
CRAI	Comptes rendus de l'Académie des Inscriptions et Belles-Lettres.
EPRO	Études preliminaires aux religions orientales dans l'Empire Romain, ed. M. J. Veramseren.
Glotta	'Glotta', Zeitschrift für greichische und lateinische Sprache.
GZMBiH	Glasnik Zemaljskog Muzeja B. i H.
HA	Histria Archaeologica.
HAD	Hrvatsko arheološko društvo.
Homm. Vermaseren	Margreet B. de Boer – T. A. (éds), *Hommages à Maarten J. Vermaseren* I-III (EPRO 68), Leiden 1978.
HSPh	Harvard Studies in Classical Philology.
HThR	Harvard Theological Studies.
ILS	Inscriptiones Latinae Selectae.
JHS	The Journal of Hellenic Studies.
JÖAI	Jahreshefte des Österreichischen Archaeologischen Instituts.
JRS	The Journal of Roman Studies.
JWCI	Journal of the Warburg and Courtlauld Institutes.
JZ	Jadranski Zbornik.
Latomus	'Latomus'. Revue d'études latines.
OA	Opuscula Archaeologica.
OZ	Osječki zbornik.
ÖJh	Jahreshefte des österreichischen archäologischen Instituts.
RA	Revue Archéologique.
RBi	Revue Biblique.
RendPont Acc	Atti della Pontificia Accademia Romana di Archeologia. Rendiconti.
RGVV	Religionsgeschichtliche Versuche und Vorarbeiten.
RHLR	Revue d'Histoire et de Littérature Religieuses.
Serta Hoffilleriana	Hoffillerov Sbornik. Commentationes gratulatorias Victori Hoffiller sexagenario obtulerunt collegae, amici, discipuli, Zagabriae 1940, (VAHD 18-19 (1937-40)).
SP	Starohrvatska prosvijeta.
SZ	Senjski Zbornik.
TAPhA	Transactions and Proceedings of the American Association.
UCPCPh	University of California. Publications in Classical Philology.
VAHD	Vjesnik za Arheologiju i Historiju Dalmatinsku.
VAMZ	Vjesnik Arheološkog Muzeja u Zagrebu.
ŽA	Živa Antika.

WORKS CITED

Abramić, M. 1929. 'Spomenici iz bedema stare Salone', *VAHD* 50 (1928/29).

——. 1940. 'Novi votivni reljefi okonjenih božanstva iz Dalmacije', *Serta Hoffilleriana* 299-302.

——. 1950. 'Tyche (Fortuna) Salonitana', *VAHD* 52 (1950), 279-289.

Albright, W. F. 1929, 'The Anatolian Goddess Kubaba', *AOF* 5 (1928 -1929), 229-231.

Alföldy, G. 1961. 'Die Stellung der Frau in der Gesellschaft der Liburner', *AASH* 9 (1961), 307-319.

——. 1963. 'Cognatio Nantania (Zur Struktur der Sippengesellschaft der Liburner) ', *AASH* 11 (1963), 81-87.

Balen, J., Demo, Ž., Ožanić, I., Radman – Livaja, I., Rendić – Miočević, A. and Uranić, I. 2003. *Na tragovima vremena, iz arheološke zbirke Mateja Pavletića*, Zagreb 2003.

Bankò, G., Sticotti, P. 1896. *Collezione di antichità nel Seminario archievescoville di Udine*, *BASD* 19 (1896).

Belamarić, J. 1998. 'The first Centuries of Christianity in Diocletian's Palace in Split', *Radovi XIII. Međunarodnog kongresa za starokršćansku arheologiju Split – Poreč (25. 9 – 1. 10. 1994) III, VAHD* Supl. 87-89, Split 1998, 55-69.

Bianchi, U. 1976. *The Greek Mysteries (Iconography of Religions XVII, 3)*, Leiden 1976.

——. ed. 1979. *Mysteria Mithrae*, Leiden 1979.

Bieber, M. 1969. 'The Images of Cybele in Roman Coins and Sculpture', J. Bibauw ed., *Hommages à Marcel Renard* (Coll. *Latomus* 103) 3, Bruxelles 1969, 29-40.

Битракова Грозданова, В. 1999. *Религија и Уметност во антиката во Македонија*, Скопје 1999.

Bonnechere, P. 2003. 'Trophonius of Lebadea: mystery aspects of an oracular cult in Boeotia', M. B. Cosmopoulos ed., *Greek Mysteries, the Archaeology and Ritual of Ancient Greek Secret Cults*, London 2003, 169-192.

Brelich, A. 1963. 'Politeismo e Soteriologia', S. G. F. Brandon (ed.), *The Saviour God. Comparative Studies in the Concept of Salvation presented to Edwin Oliver James,* Manchester 1963, 37-50.

Brouwer, H. H. J. 1978. 'The Great Mother and the Good Goddess. The History of Identification.', *Homm. Vermaseren* I, EPRO 68, Leiden 1978, 142-159.

Brunšmid, J. 1909. 'Kameni spomenici hrvatskoga narodnoga muzeja u Zagrebu III', *VHAD* 10 (1908-1909), 163-164.

——. 1914. 'Antikni bronzani figuralni predmeti u Hrvatskom narodnom muzeju u Zagrebu', *VHAD* 13 (1913-1914).

Budischovsky, M. C. 1977. 'Les Cultes orientaux a Aquilee et leur diffusion en Istrie en Venetie', Aquileia e l' Oriente Mediterreneo, *Antichita Altoadriatiche* 12 (1977), 99-123.

Bulat, M. 1997. 'Spomenici kulta Kabira iz Osijeka', *OZ* 22-23 (1997), 21-32.

Burkert, W. 1977. *Greek Religion, Archaic and Classical,* Harvard University Press 1977.

——. 1979. *Structure and History in Greek Mythology and Ritual,* London 1979.

——. 1983. *Homo Necans: The Anthropology of Ancient Greek Sacrificial Ritual and Myth,* trans. P. Bing, Berkeley 1983.

——. 1987a. *Ancient Mystery Cults,* London 1987.

——. 1987b. 'Oriental and Greek Mythology: The Meeting of Parallels', Bremmer, J. ed. *Interpretations of Greek Mythology,* London 1987, 10-40.

——. 2004. *Babylon, Memphis, Persepolis. Eastern Contexts of Greek Culture.* Harvard University Press 2004.

Cambi, N. 1960. 'Personifikacije godišnjih doba na spomenicima Salone', *VAHD* 62 (1960).

——. 1965. 'Ženski likovi s krunom u obliku gradskih zidina iz srednje Dalmacije', *VAHD* 65-67 (1963-1965), 55-68.

——. 1968. 'Silvan – Atis, primjer kultnog sinkretizma', *Diadora* 4 (1968), 131-141.

——. 1970. 'La figure du Christ sur les monuments pléochrétiens de Dalmatie', *Disp. Salonitanae I*, 1970.

——. 1977. 'Krist i njegova simbolika u likovnoj umjetnosti strarokršćanskog perioda u Dalmaciji', *VAHD* 70-71 (1977), 57-106.

——. 1980. 'Trogir u antici', *Mogućnosti* 27 (1980).

——. 1993. 'Bilješke uz kipove Kibele (Magna Mater) iz Senja', *SZ* 20 (1993), 33-44.

——. 2002. *Antika*, Zagreb 2002.

——. 2003. 'Attis or someone else on funerary monuments from Dalmatia?', *Akten des VII. Internationalen Colloquiums über Probleme des provinzialrömischen Kunstschaffens*, Mainz am Rhein 2003, 511-520.

——. 2005a. 'Funerary Monuments from Dalmatia, Istria and the Croatian Part of Panonnia. A Comparative Study', M. Sanader, A. Rendić Miočević ured., *Akti VIII. Međunarodnog Kolokvija o problemima rimskog provincijalnog umjetničkog stvaralaštva*, Zagreb 5.-8. V. 2003., Zagreb 2005, 13-30.

——. 2005b. *Kiparstvo rimske Dalmacije*, Split 2005.

Carcopino, J. 1926. 'Note sur une inscription métroaque récemment découverte', *RendPontAcc* IV (1925-1926), 231-246.

Carli, J. R. 1794. *Delle antichità Italiche II*, Milano 1794.

Chantraine, P. 1968. *Dictionnaire étymologique de la langue grecque I*, 1968.

Clinton, K. 2003. 'Stages of Initiation in the Eleusinian and Samothracian Mysteries', M. B. Cosmopoulos ed., *Greek Mysteries, the Archaeology and Ritual of Ancient Greek Secret Cults*, London 2003, 50-78.

Cole, S. G. 1984. *Theoi Megaloi: The Cult of the Great Gods at Samothrace*, EPRO 96, Leiden 1984.

Cosmopoulos, M. B. 2003. 'Concluding Remarks', M. B. Cosmopoulos ed. *Greek Mysteries, the Archaeology and Ritual of Ancient Greek Secret Cults*, London 2003, 263-264.

Cumont, F. 1888. 'Le taurobole et le culte de Anahita', *RA* 12 (1888), 132 – 136.

———. 1901. 'Le taurobole et le culte de Bellone', *RHLR* 6 (1901), 97 – 110.

———. 1914. *Die orientalischen Religionen im Römischen Heidentum*, Leipzig – Berlin 1914.

———. 1942. *Recherches sur le Symbolisme Funéraire des Romains*, Paris 1942.

Čače, S. 1985. *Liburnija u razdoblju od 4. do 1. stoljeća prije nove ere*, Disertation, Zadar 1985.

Degmedžić, I. 1952. 'Arheološka Istraživanja u Senju', *VAHD* 53 (1952), 251-262.

Degrassi, A. 1933. 'Valdarsa, dedica alla *Mater Magna Deorum*', *Notizie degli scavi* 1933.

———. 1936. *Inscriptiones Italiae, 10/3, Histria Septemtrionalis*, Roma 1936.

———. 1970. 'Culti dell' Istria Preromana e Romana', *Adriatica Praehistorica et Antiqua – Miscellanea Gregoriia Novak*, Zagreb 1970, 615-632.

Dessau, H. 1916. *ILS* I-III, Berlin 1892-1916.

Diakonoff, I. M. 1977, 'On Cybele and Attis in Phrygia and Lydia', *AASH* 25 (1977), 333-340.

Dobruna – Salihu, E. 2005. 'Cult Symbols and Images on Funerary Monuments of the Roman Period in the Central Section of Dardania', M. Sanader, A. Rendić Miočević ed., *Akti VIII. Međunarodnog Kolokvija o problemima rimskog provincijalnog umjetničkog stvaralaštva, Zagreb 5.-8. V. 2003.*, Zagreb 2005, 343 – 350.

Dodig, R. 2005. 'Afterlife Ideas on Military Monuments in Narona Hinterland', M. Sanader, A. Rendić Miočević eds., *Akti VIII. Međunarodnog Kolokvija o problemima rimskog provincijalnog umjetničkog stvaralaštva, Zagreb 5.-8. V. 2003.*, Zagreb 2005, 205-212.

Dodds, E. R. 1956. *The Greeks and the Irational*, Berkeley 1956.

Dölger, F. J. 1922, *Der Heilige Fisch in den Antiken Religionen und im Christentum II*, Münster 1922.

Duthoy, R. 1966. 'La Minerva Berecyntia des inscriptions tauroboliques de Bénévent', *AC* 35 (1966), 548-561.

———. 1968. 'Traces archéologiques de tauroboles à Zadar?', *Latomus* 27 (1968), 622-629.

———. 1969. *The Taurobolium, its Evolution and Terminology*, EPRO 10, Leiden 1969.

Dyggve, E. 1951. *Hystory of Salonitan Christianity*, Oslo 1951.

Fadić, I. 2003. 'Novi liburnijski cipusi iz Aserije', *Asseria*, Zadar 2003, 97-131.

Fauth, W. 1967. 'Adamma Kubaba', *Glotta* 45 (1967), 129-148.

Fear, A. T. 1996. 'Cybelle and Christ', Lane, E. ed., *Cybelle, Attis and related Cults*, Essays in Memory of M.J. Vermaseren, Brill 1996, 37-50.

Fishwick, D. 1966. 'The Cannophori and the March Festival of Magna Mater', *TAPhA* 97 (1966), 193-202.

———. 1967. 'Hastiferi', *JRS* 57 (1967), 142-160.

Frankfurter, S. 1884. *Epigraphischer Bericht aus Oestereich, Dalmatia in AEMO* 8 1884, 104-128.

Garašanin, M. and D. 1951. *Arheološka nalazišta u Srbiji*, Beograd 1951.

Gimbutas, M. 1989. *The Language of the Goddess*, New York 1989.

Girardi - Jurkić, V. 1972. 'Rasprostranjenost Kulta Magnae Matris na Području Istre u Rimsko Doba', *HA* 3/1 (1972), 41-59.

———. 1978. 'Skulptura Atisa iz Pule' *JZ* 10 (1978), 174-188.

———. 1979. 'Kultovi Plodnosti na području antičke Istre', *Građa i Rasprave* 8, Pula 1979, 37-47.

———. 1999. *Kultovi u procesu romanizacije antičke Istre*, Disertacija, Zagreb 1999.

———. 2005. 'Reliefs and Sculptures of Dieties and mythological Representation as Determining Factors of the Spiritual Life in antique Pula', M. Sanader, A. Rendić Miočević eds., *Akti VIII. Međunarodnog Kolokvija o problemima rimskog provincijalnog umjetničkog stvaralaštva, Zagreb 5.-8. V. 2003.*, Zagreb 2005, 191-195.

Gjurašin, H. 1989. *Vodič, Brački muzej Škrip, O desetoj godišnjici djelovanja Bračkog muzeja 1979 – 1989*, Zagreb – Supetar 1989.

———. 1990. 'Kasnoantički nalazi iz Škripa na otoku Braču i srebrni prsten iz Vrlike', *SP* 20, ser. 3, Split 1990, 251-263.

Glavičić, M., 1968. 'Arheološki nalazi iz Senja i Okolice (II)', *SZ* 3 (1967-1968),5-35.

———. 1994. 'Natpisi antičke Senije', *Radovi Filozofskog fakulteta u Zadru* 33, Razdio povijesnih znanosti (20) 1993/1994, Zadar 1994, 55-82.

———. 2005. 'Kultskulpturen aus der antiken Stadt Senia' M. Sanader, A. Rendić Miočević eds., *Akti VIII. Međunarodnog Kolokvija o problemima rimskog provincijalnog umjetničkog stvaralaštva, Zagreb 5.-8. V. 2003.*, Zagreb 2005, 223-228.

Gnirs, A. 1912. 'Grabungen im südlichen Istrien', *JÖAI* 15 (1912), 5 -16.

———. 1915. *Pula. Ein Führer durch di antike Baudenkmäler und Sammlungen*, Wien 1915.

Gorenc, M. 1952. *Antikna skulptura u Hrvatskoj*, Zagreb 1952.

Graff, F. 2003. 'Lesser Mysteries – not less mysterious', M. B. Cosmopoulos ed. *Greek Mysteries, the Archaeology and Ritual of Ancient Greek Secret Cults*, London 2003, 241-262.

Graillot, H. 1912. *Le culte de Cybèle Mère des Dieux à Rome et dans l'Empire romaine*, Paris 1912.

———. 1912b. 'Mater deum salutaris. Cybèle protectrice des eaux thermals', *Mélanges Capart*, Paris 1912.

Gregl, Z. 1996. 'Sadržaj antiknih kamenih spomenika nađenih u Zagrebu i okolici II', *Iz starog i novog Zagreba* 7 (1996), 9 – 18.

Gregl, Z., Migotti, B. 2000. 'Nadgrobna stela iz Siska', *VAMZ* 3/32-33 (1999-2000), 119 – 164.

Gruen, E., 1990. 'The Advebt of Magna Mater', *Studies of Greek Culture and Roman Policy*, 1990, 5-33.

Hadzisteliou Price, Th. 1971. 'Double and Multiple Representations in Greek Art and Religious Thought', *JHS* 91 (1971), 48-69.

——. 1978. *Kourotrophos, Cults and Representations of the Greek Nursing Deities*, Leiden 1987.

Hemberg, B. 1950. *Die Kabiren*, Uppsala 1950.

Hepding, H. 1903. *Attis, seine Mythen und sein Kult*, RGVV I, Gieszen 1903.

Hofman, H. 1905. *Römische Militärgrabsteine der Donauländer*, Wien 1905.

Iskra – Janošić, I. 1966. 'Rimske votivne pločice od olova u Jugoslaviji', *OA* 6 (1966), 48 – 69, T. I - VI.

Iveković, Č. 1910. *Dalmatiens Architektur und Plastik VI – VIII*, Wien 1910.

Jelić, L. 1894. *Guida di Spalato e Salona*, Split 1894.

Jobst, H. 1998. 'The Cult of the Oriental Dieties in Canuntum', *Religions and Cults in Pannonia, Exhibition at Székestehérvár, Csók István Gallery, 15 May – 30 September 1996*, Székestehérvár 1998, 37 - 42.

Jurkić, V. 1972. 'Portreti na nadgrobnim stelama zbirke antičkog odjela Arheološkog muzeja Istre u Puli', *JZ* vol.8 (1972), 359-382.

——. 1975. 'The Cult of Magna Mater in the Region of Istra', *ŽA*, 1/2 (1975), 285-298.

——. 1976. 'Izbor antičke kultne plastike na području istre', *Materijali* 12, Zadar 1976, 209-223.

——. 1978. 'Skulptura Attisa iz Pule', *JZ* 10 (1978),174-188.

Kandler, P. 1855. 'Iscrizioni romane dell'Istria', *Indicazioni per riconoscere le cose storiche del Litorale*, Trieste 1855.

Katančić, M. P. 1826. *Istri adcolarum vetus e monumentis epigraphicis, marmoribus, numis, tabellis eruta et commentariis illustrata a p. M. P. Katancsich o. m. P. F. prov. capistr. AA. LL. et philos. doct. in reg. univers. hung. antiquit. ac numism. prof. et biblioth. cust. emerit.* I, Budae 1826.

Katičić, B. 1995. *Illyricum Mythologicum*, Zagreb 1995.

Koščević, R. 2000. *Arheološka zbirka Benko Horvat*, Zagreb 2000.

Kovač, L. 1992. 'Nezakcijski kult – simboličke forme i njihove transformacije od 6. st. pr. n. e. do 6. st. n. e.', *HA* 22 – 23 (1991-2), 44-116.

Kubitschek, G. 1896. 'Il culto della Mater Magna in Salona', *Bullettino di archeologia e storia dalmata*, 19, 1896, 87-89.

Kukoč, S. 1993. 'Histarska plastika u kontekstu umjetnosti jadranskog područja od 7. do 5. stoljeća pr. n. e.', *Radovi Filozofskog fakulteta u Zadru* 26 (139) 1987.

Kulenović, I., Muštra, M. 2002. 'Novi nalaz kruništa s lavljim parom s lokaliteta Gabajeva greda kod Koprivnice', *OA* 26 (2002), 143 – 152.

Kukuljević. I. 1873. *Rad Jugoslovenske Akademije Znanosti i Umjetnosti* 23, Zagreb 1873.

Kuntić - Makvić, B. 1982. 'Žrtvenik iz Varvarije posvećen božici Izidi', *Arheološki radovi i rasprave* 8 – 9 (1982) Zagreb, 151 – 157.

——. 1994. 'Pretkršćanski zaštitnici', *Sveti Vlaho poglaviti dubrovački obranitelj*, Dubrovnik n. s. 5/5 1994, 22 - 28.

——. 2000. 'Kako preseliti hram', *OA* 23-24 (2000), 115-122.

Kurilić, A. 1995. 'Obitelj u ranorimskoj Liburniji', Radovi FFZd, *Razdio povijesnih znanosti* 21 (1994/5), 47 – 83.

Lagrange, M. - J. 1919. 'Mélanges I. Attis et le christianisme', *RBi* 28, 1919.

Lancellotti, M. G. 2002. *Attis, Between Myth and Hystory: King, Priest and God*, Religions in the Graeco - Roman World, 149, Leiden 2002.

Landskron, A. 2005. 'Attis, Parther und andere Barbaren. Ein Beitrag zum Verständnis von Orientalendarstellungen auf Grabsteinen der Nördlichen Provinzen', M. Sanader, A. Rendić Miočević eds., *Akti VIII. Međunarodnog Kolokvija o problemima rimskog provincijalnog umjetničkog stvaralaštva, Zagreb 5.-8. V. 2003.*, Zagreb 2005, 121-130.

Lane, E. 1976. CMRDM I – III, EPRO 19, Leiden 1971 – 76.

Lanza, F. 1855. *Del antico Palazzo di Diocleziano*, Trieste 1855.

___. 1856. *Monumenti Salonitani Inediti*, Viena 1856.

Lawall, M. L. 2003. 'In the Sanctuary of the Samothracian Gods: myth, politics, and mystery cult at Ilion', M. B. Cosmopoulos ed., *Greek Mysteries, the Archaeology and Ritual of Ancient Greek Secret Cults*, London 2003, 79- 111.

Lewis, I. M., 1971. *Ecstatic Religion. An Antropological Study of Spirit Possession and Shamanism*, Penguin books 1971.

Linforth, I. M. 1946. 'The Corybantic Rites in Plato', *UCPCPh* 13, 5 (1946), 121-162.

Marasović, J. and T. 1968. *Dioklecijanova palača*, Zagreb 1968.

Marasović, T. 1994. *Dioklecijanova palača*, Zagreb 1994.

Маразов, И. 1992. *Мит, Ритуал и Изкуство у Траките*, София 1992.

——. 1994. *Митологија на Траките*, Софија 1994.

Марић, Р. 1933. *Антички култови у нашој земљи*, Београд 1933.

Medini, J. 1967. 'Epigrafički podaci o munificencijama i ostalim javnim gradnjama iz antičke Liburnije', *Radovi Filozofskog fakulteta u Zagrebu* 6, Razdio historije, arheologije i historije umjetnosti 3, Zadar 1967, 45-74.

——. 1968. 'Rimska brončana plastika u Arheološkom muzeju u Zadru', *Diadora* 4, Zadar 1968, 143-160.

——. 1977. 'Spomenik Atisova kulta iz Medviđe', *Radovi Filozofskog fakulteta u Zadru* 16, Razdio društvenih znanosti (7)/1976/1977, Zadar 1977, 195-205.

——. 1978. 'Le culte de Cybèle dans la Liburnie antique', *Homm Vermaseren* II, 732 – 756.

——. 1980. 'Sabazijev kult u rimskoj provinciji Dalmaciji', *VAHD* 74 (1980), 67-88.

——. 1981a. 'Salonitanski arhigalat', *Radovi Fil. Fak. Zadar (Razd. društv. zn.)* 20 (9) (1980-81), 15-28.

——. 1981b. *Maloazijske religije u rimskoj provinciji Dalmaciji*, Disertacija, Zadar 1981.

——. 1984a, 'Spomenici s Atisovim likom na području Sinjske krajine', *Cetinska krajina od prethistorije do dolaska Turaka*, HAD, sv. 8, Split 1984, 107-126.

—. 1984b. 'Latra – dea Neditarum', Simpozijum 'Duhovna kultura Ilira', *Posebna izdanja ANUBiH*, Centar za balkanološka ispitivanja 67/11, Sarajevo 1984, 223-244.

—. 1985. 'Cognationes Salonitanae', Godišnjak 23, Centar za balkanološka ispitivanja 21 (1985), 5-43.

—. 1986. 'Aplike u obliku Atisove glave iz rimske provincije Dalmacije', *Radovi Filozofskog fakulteta u Zadru* 25, *Razdio povijesnih znanosti* (12)/1985/1986, Zadar 1986, 109-125.

—. 1989a. 'Metroaca Burnensia', *Diadora* 11 (1989), 255-284.

—. 1989b. 'Metroačka religija u Aenoni', *Radovi Filozofskog fakulteta u Zadru* 28, *Razdio povijesnih znanosti* (15)/1988/1989, Zadar 1989, 19-31.

—. 1993. 'Kult Kibele u antičkoj Liburniji', *SZ* 20 (1993), 1-32.

Mellaart, J. 1963. 'Excavations at Çatal Hüyük, 1962, Second preliminary Report', *AS* 13 (1963).

—. 1967. *Çatal Hüyük. A neolitic town in Anatolia*, London 1967.

Meskell, L. 1998. 'Twin Peaks', Goodison, L.; Morris, C. eds., *Ancient Goddesses, The Myths and the Evidence*, London 1998, 46-62.

Miletić, Ž. 1966. *Mitraizm u rimskoj provinciji Dalmaciji*, Dissertation, Zadar 1996.

Mitropoulou, E. 1996. 'The Goddess Cybele in funerary Banquets and with an Equestrian Hero', Lane, E. ed., *Cybele, Attis and related Cults*, Essays in Memory of M.J. Vermaseren, Brill 1996, 135-165.

Mlakar, Š. 1978. 'Antička izložba', *Arheološki muzej Istre (vodič III)*, Pula 1978.

Moore, C. H. 1906. 'On the Origin of the Taurobolium', *HSPh* 27 (1906), 43-48.

—. 1924. 'The Duration of the Efficacy of the Taurobolium', *CPh* 19 (1924), 363-365.

Musso, L. 1983. *Manifattura Suntuaria e Committenza Pagana nella Roma del IV Secolo: Indagine sulla Lanx di Parabiago*, Roma 1983.

Nardelli, B. 1989. 'Terakotna plastika u Arheološkome muzeju u Splitu', *VAHD* 82 (1989), 35-123.

Naumann, F. 1983. *Die Ikonographie der Kybele in der Phrygischen und der Griechischen Kunst*, Istanbuler Mitteilungen, Beihaft 28, Tübingen 1983.

Nilsson, M. 1963. *A History of Greek Religion*, Oxford 1963.

Nock, A. D. 1952. 'Hellenistic Mysteries and Christian Sacraments', *Mnemosyne* 5 (1952), 177-213.

Patsch, C. 1908. 'Kleinere Untersuchungen in und um Narona', *Jahrbuch für Altertumstkunde II*, Wien 1908, 105.

Петрова, Е. 1996. *Бригите на централниот Балкан во II и I милениум пред н. е.*, Скопје 1996.

Pinterović, D. 1967a. '*Mursa* u svjetlu novih izvora i nove literature', *OZ* 11 (1967), 23-65.

—. 1967b. 'Nove Rimske skulpture u muzeju Slavonije', *OZ* 11 (1967), 67-79.

—. 1975. 'Nepoznata Slavonija', *OZ* 14-15 (1975), 123-166.

Popović, Lj. B., Mano Zisi, D., Veličković, M. and Jeličić, B. 1963. *Antička bronza u Jugoslaviji*, Beograd 1969.

Reichel, G. 1893. 'Beschreibung der Sculpturen im Augustustempel in Pula', *AEMO* 16 (1893), 1 – 13.

Rein, M. J. 1996. 'Phrygian Matar: Emergence of an Iconographic Type', Lane, E. ed. *Cybele, Attis and related Cults*, Essays in Memory of M.J.Vermaseren, Brill 1996, 223-237.

Reisch, E. 1913. 'Das Standlager von *BURNUM*', *JÖAI* 16 (1913), 119 – 121.

Reitzenstein, R. 1987. *Hellenistic Mystery Religions, their basic Ideas and Significance*, trans. J. E. Steely, Pittsburgh 1978.

Rendić – Miočević, D. 1960. 'Ilirske onomastičke studije', *ŽA* 10 (1960), 165-168.

—. 1989. *Iliri i antički svijet*, Split 1989.

Rendić – Miočević, A. 1993. 'Rimska nadgrobna stela iz Odre nadomak Zagreba', *ObHAD* 25/2 (1993), 28-31.

Rendić – Miočević, A. and Šegvić, M. 1998. 'Religions and Cults in south Pannonian Regions', *Religions and Cults in Pannonia*, Exhibition at Székestehérvár, Csók István Gallery, 15 May – 30 September 1996, Székestehérvár 1998.

Righini V. 1965. 'Forma e struttura delle porte romane: Gli esemplari di Sarsina', *Studi Romagnoli* 16 (1965).

Robert, L. 1955. 'Dedicaces et reliefs votifs. 14. Meter Therméné', *Helenica* 10 (1955), 78-82, Pl. XXI, 2.

—. 1975. 'Une nouvelle inscription grecque de Sardes: Règlement de l'autorité perse relatif à un culte de Zeus', *CRAI* (1975), 306-330.

Robertson, N. 1996. 'The ancient Mother of the Gods, a missing Chapter in the History of Greek Religion', Lane, E. ed., *Cybelle, Attis and related Cults*, Essays in Memory of M. J. Vermaseren, Brill 1996, 239-304.

—. 2003. 'Orphic Mysteries and Dionysiac Ritual', M. B. Cosmopoulos ed., *Greek Mysteries, the Archaeology and Ritual of Ancient Greek Secret Cults*, London 2003, 218-240.

Sanader, M. 2003. 'Grabsteine der *Legio VII* aus *Tilurium* – Versuch einer Typologie', *Akten des VII. Internationalen Colloquiums über Probleme des provinzialrömischen Kunstschaffens*, Mainz am Rhein 2003, 501- 510.

Sanders, G. 1981. 'Kybele und Attis', M. J. Vermaseren ed., *Die orientalischen Religionen im Römerreich* (OrRR), EPRO 93, Leiden 1981, 264- 297.

Sako, Z. 1972. 'De la genèse de la danse pyrrhique', *Studia Albanica* 9 (1972), 307-310.

Schachter, A. 2003. 'Evolutions of a Mystery Cult. The Theban Kabiroi', M. B. Cosmopoulos ed., *Greek Mysteries, the Archaeology and Ritual of Ancient Greek Secret Cults*, London 2003, 112-142.

Schillinger, K. 1979. *Untersuchungen zur Entwicklung des Magna Mater – Kultes im Western des römischen Kaiserreiches*, Konstanz 1979.

Schober, A. 1923. *Die römischen Grabsteine von Noricum und Pannonien*, Wien 1923.

Schwertheim, E. 1976. 'Denkmäler zur Meretverehrung in Bithynien und Mysien', S. Şahin; E. Schwertheim; J. Wagner, ed., *Studien zur Religionen und Kultur Kleinasiens*, Festschrift für Friedrich Karl Dörner zum 65. Geburtstag am 28 Februar 1976, EPRO 66, Leiden 1976, vol II, 791-837.

Selem, P. 1972. *Egipatski bogovi u rimskom Iliriku*, Sarajevo 1972.

——. 1980. *Les religions orientales dans la Pannonie Romaine. Partie en Yougoslavie*, Leiden 1980.

——. 1981. 'Aspekti teatralizacije u Kultu Kybele i Attisa', *Antički teatar na tlu Jugoslavije, Saopštenja sa naučnog skupa 14.-17. april 1980, Novi Sad 1981*, 189-198.

——. 2005. 'Quelques indices sur les relations entre les divinités autochtones et orientales en Dalmatie romaine', *Illyrica Antiqua*, Zagreb 2005, 425-432.

Sergejevski, D. 1934. 'Rimska groblja na Drini', *GZMBiH* 46 (1934), 11-36.

Sfameni Gasparro, G. 1983. 'Significato e ruolo del sangue nel culto di Cibele e Attis', *Atti della Settimana di Studi 'Sangue e antropologia biblica nella letteratura cristiana'*, Roma, 29 novembre-4 dicemre 1982, cur. F. Vattioni, Roma 1983, vol.I, 199-232.

——. 1985. *Soteriology and Mystic Aspects in the Cult of Cybele and Attis*, EPRO, Leiden 1985.

——. 1966. 'Per la Storia del Culto di Cibele in Occidente: Il Santuario Rupestre di Akrai', Lane, E. ed. *Cybele, Attis and related Cults*, Essays in Memory of M.J.Vermaseren, Brill 1996, 51-86.

Starac, A. *Rimsko vladanje u Histriji i Liburniji I*, Pula 1999.

Sticotti, P. 1914. 'Nuova rassegna di epigrafi romane', *AMSI* 30 (1914), 87-134.

——. 1934. 'Scavo di Nesazio, Campagna del 1922', *AMSI* 46 (1934).

Stipčević, A. 1974. *Iliri*, Zagreb 1974.

Suić, M. 1952. 'Liburnijski nadgrobni cipus', *VAHD* 53 (1952).

——. 1965a. 'Peintures romaines récemment trouvées à Zadar', *Huitième Congrés international d'archéologie classique*, Paris 1965, 353 – 355, Pl. 74, 75.

——. 1965b. 'Orijentalni Kultovi u antičkom Zadru', *Diadora* 3, 1965, 91-128.

——. 1966. 'Iz mediteranske Baštine jadranskih Ilira', *Radovi Filozofskog fakulteta u Zadru* 4, Razdio historije, arheologije i historije umjetnosti (2)/1962/1963, Zadar 1966, 44-58.

——. 1981. *Zadar u starom vijeku*, Zadar 1981.

Summers, K. 1996. 'Lucretius' Roman Cybele', Lane, E. ed. *Cybele, Attis and related Cults*, Essays in Memory of M.J.Vermaseren, Brill 1996, 337-365.

Susini, G. 1978. 'I Culti orientali nella Cispadana', *Homm. Vermaseren* III, EPRO 68, Leiden 1978, 1199 - 1216.

——. 1985. 'Scritura e produzione culturale: dal dossier romano di Sarsina', *Cultura epigrafica* dell'Appennino. Faenza 1985, 86-88.

Swoboda, R. M. 1969. 'Denkmäler des Mater-Magna-Kultes in Slowenien und Istrien', *BJ* 169 (1969), 195-207.

Šašel Kos, M. 1993. 'Cadmus and Harmonia in Illyria', *Arh. Vest.* 44 (1993), 113-136.

——. 1999. *Pre-Roman Divinities of the Eastern Alps and Adriatic*, Ljubljana 1999.

Thomas, G. 1984. 'Magna Mater and Attis', *ANRW* II, 17.3 (1984), 1500-1535.

Tončinić, D. 2004. *Spomenici VII. Legije na području rimske provincije Dalmacije*, Magistarski rad, Zagreb 2004.

Tóth, I. 1989. 'The Remains of the Cult of Magna Mater and Attis in Pannonia', *Specimina Nova*, 1989.

Tudor, D. 1960. 'Nuovi monumenti sui Cavalieri danubiani: Addenda' *Dacia* N. S. 4 (1960), 445 – 449.

——. 1969. CMRED I, *The Monuments*, Leiden 1969.

——. 1976. CMRED II, *The Analysis and Interpretation of the Monuments*, Leiden 1976.

Turcan, R., 1996a. 'Attis Platonicus', Lane, E., ed., *Cybelle, Attis and related Cults*, Essays in Memory of M. J. Vermaseren, Brill 1996, 387-403.

——. 1996b. *The Cults of the Roman Empire*, trans. A. Nevill, Blackwell Publishing 1996.

Vermaseren, M. J. 1966. *The Legend of Attis in Greek and Roman Art*, EPRO 9, Leiden 1966.

——. 1974. 'Kybele und Attis mit dem Fisch', *In Memoriam Constantini Davicoviciu*, Cluj 1974, 401-408.

——. 1976. 'Kybele und Merkur', S. Şahin; E. Schwertheim; J. Wagner, ed., *Studien zur Religionen und Kultur Kleinasiens*, Festschrift für Friedrich Karl Dörner zum 65. Geburtstag am 28 Februar 1976, EPRO 66 II, Leiden 1976, 956-966.

——. 1977a. *Cybele and Attis, the Myth and the Cult*, London 1977.

——. 1977b. CCCA VII, *Musea et Collectiones privatae*, EPRO 50, Leiden 1977.

——. 1977c. CCCA III, *Italia - Latium*, EPRO 50, Leiden 1977.

——. 1978. CCCA IV, *Italia – Aliae Provinciae*, EPRO 50, Leiden 1978.

——. 1982. CCCA II, *Graecia atque insulae*, EPRO 50, Leiden 1982.

——. 1986. CCCA V, *Aegyptus, Africa, Hispania, Gallia et Britannia*, EPRO 50, Leiden 1986.

——. 1987. CCCA I, *Asia Minor*, EPRO 50, Leiden 1987.

——. 1989. CCCA VI, *Germania, Raetia, Noricum, Pannonia, Dalmatia, Macedonia, Thracia, Moesia, Dacia, Regnum Bospori, Colchis, Scythia et Sarmatia*, EPRO 50, Leiden 1989.

Versnel, H. S. 1987. 'Greek Myth and Ritual: The Case of Kronos', Bremmer, J. ed, *Interpretations of Greek Mythology*, London 1987, 121-152.

Waldmann, H. 1978. 'Ein Archimystes in Salagassos', *Homm Vermaseren* III 1978, 1309 – 1315.

Waltzing, J. P. 1899. *Étude historique sur les corporations professionelles chez les Romains* III, Recueil des inscriptions greques et latines relatives aux corporations des Romains, Louvain 1899.

Weisshäupl, R. 1901. 'Zur Topographie des alten Pula', *JÖAI* 4 (1901), 169-208.

Welch, K. 1996. 'A Statue Head of the *Great Mother* from Samotrace', *Hesperia* 65/4 (October – December 1996), 467 – 473, Tab. 89-92.

Wenzel, M. 1961. 'A Medieval Mystery Cult in Bosnia and Herzegovina', *JWCI* 24 (1961).

Will, E. 1955. *Le Relief cultuel gréco – romain*. Contribution à l'historie de l'art de l'empire romain, Paris 1955, 315, fig. 63.

Zotović, M. 1973. 'Jugozapadna Srbija u doba Rimljana', *Užički zbornik* 2 (1973).

Zuntz, G. 1971. *Persephone, Three Essays on Religion and Thought in Magna Graecia,* Oxford 1971.

Žanić-Protić, J. 1988. 'Antička brončana plastika iz Arheološkog Muzeja u Splitu I.', *VAHD* 81 (1988), 21-32.

www.ingramcontent.com/pod-product-compliance
Lightning Source LLC
Chambersburg PA
CBHW060840010526
44108CB00050B/2890